MW01228489

DEFEATING JEZEBEL

OVERCOMING FEAR AND ANXIETY

BY ZAKIYA ROBINSON

Scripture is taking from the King James Bible, Full Color edition Copyright 1988, 2013, 2017, by Liberty University.

Scripture is taking from KJV/Amplified Side By Side, Copyright 2015, by The Lockman Foundation.

Scripture is taking from Holy Bible, New Living Translation, Copyright 1996, 2004, 2015, by Tyndale House Foundation.

Copyright © 2023 by Zakiya Robinson
All rights reserved. No parts of this publication may be reproduced, distributed, or transmitted in any form or by any means, including photocopying, recording, or other electronic or mechanical methods without the prior written permission of the author..

Dedication

I dedicate this book to many influential people who have helped me through my healing. First is to the Holy Spirit for guiding me into the woman I am today. With the leading of the Holy Spirit, this book was able to be done, and revelation was given. Thank you to my husband for supporting my book-writing journey and motivating me to publish what God has placed on my heart. You are my better half that keeps me on the right path and keeps me with fresh revelation. I would also like to thank my mother and father for their love and support.

Lastly, Thank you to my five kids, Terry, Tyler, Aaliyah, Tyson, and Zuri, who have helped me be the woman and mother I am and showed me that there is love beyond self. I love all of you, and I'm thankful for everyone who's helped me along the way.

CONTENTS

Introduction

W ho is Jezebel, you ask? Jezebel can be your worst enemy if you allow her to be. I will relate to Jezebel as a "SHE" since Jezebel is called a "SHE" in the Bible. Please understand that Jezebel is a spirit and can also operate in men. But for the sake of this book, I will use "SHE." Also, in this book, I will give personal experiences that I or someone else have gone through to understand better how this spirit operates in today's world. I will change the names of the people so their identity is kept private. However, I will not change the experience. Lastly, scriptures will be given and will mostly come from AMP (Amplified Bible Version). I want the reader to understand how to defeat this spirit entirely, and reading the AMP scriptures will make this book come alive and relatable.

When reading the Bible, we will apply the word of God to our lives today. With the world and events changing every year, we must learn to study how the word applies to us in our current situations. Everything we go through in life is for the glory of the Lord and personal growth. While going through these experiences, I realized that I had a lot to change about myself and that one main change was fear.

Jezebel comes to steal, kill, and destroy *(Read John 10:10)*. God's word says in

EPHESIANS 6:12-17 AMP

> [12] *For our struggle is not against flesh and blood [contending only with physical opponents], but against the rulers, against the powers, against the world forces of this [present] darkness, against the spiritual forces of wickedness in the heavenly (supernatural) places.* [13] *Therefore, put on the complete armor of God, so that you will be able to [successfully] resist and stand your ground in the evil day [of danger], and having done everything [that the crisis demands], to stand firm [in your place, fully prepared, immovable, victorious].* [14] *So stand firm and hold your ground, having] tightened the wide band of truth (personal integrity, moral courage) around your waist and having put on the breastplate of righteousness (an upright heart),* [15] *and having strapped on your feet the gospel of peace in preparation [to face the enemy with firm-footed stability and the readiness produced by the good news].* [16] *Above all, lift up the [protective] shield of faith with which you can extinguish all the flaming arrows of the evil one.* [17] *And take the helmet of salvation, and the sword of the Spirit, which is the Word of God.*

In today's time, Jezebel is running rampant. In the news, war, social media, families, marriages/relationships, your mind, church, workplaces, and in movies and shows. Everywhere you look, you will see Jezebel. She also causes confusion, separation, insecurities, doubt, jealousy, hatred, envy, and misunderstanding. Jezebel is a liar, murderer, manipulator, controlling, dominant, never satisfied, and evil. Jezebel can cause you to question God, run from your calling, commit suicide, murder, and worship false gods. Jezebel can also cause you to be lustful, controlling, have addictions, hateful, selfish, and a liar.

Jezebel is one of the strongest demons mentioned in the Bible, and if you don't have the proper tools to fight this demon, you will lose control in every area of your life. This spirit sucks the life out of you and will squeeze you like a snake squeezes its prey. This spirit can leave you lifeless, depressed, hopeless, sad, grieved, and scared.

Through the personal experiences I encountered, I had to learn to put on the full armor of God daily and to fight my battles in the spiritual rather than in the natural realms. A lot of people make the mistake of fighting spiritual battles in the flesh. Our battles start in the spiritual realm, and once you gain that understanding, you will be ahead of the devil and his demons.

Jezebel promotes fear in her victims. When she succeeds in promoting fear, she can get you off course with God and His word. This spirit will cause you to run from your calling and will cause you to hide in places God never intended you to hide. God said that we are not allowed to tolerate this spirit.

REVELATION 2:20-23 AMP

> [20] But I have this [charge] against you, that you tolerate the woman Jezebel, who calls herself a prophetess [claiming to be inspired], and she teaches and misleads My bond-servants so that they commit [acts of sexual] immorality and eat food sacrificed to idols. [21] I gave her time to repent [to change her inner self and her sinful way of thinking], but she has no desire to repent of her immorality and refuses to do so. [22] Listen carefully, I will throw her on a bed of sickness, and those who commit adultery with her [I will bring] into great anguish, unless they repent of her deeds. [23] And I will kill her children (followers) with pestilence [thoroughly annihilating them], and all the churches will know [without any doubt] that I am He who searches the] minds and hearts [the innermost thoughts, purposes]; and I will give to each one of you [a reward or punishment] according to your deeds.

We are to stand up and fight and bring her down, just like Jehu, which we will later discuss.

No more running, no more hiding, and no more fear. God's word says in *2 Timothy 1:7* **AMP**

For God hath not given us the spirit of fear; but of power, and of love, and of a sound mind.

If God has not given us the spirit of fear, then the fear came from another source. That's the devil, lucifer. God has given us the power to fight this overwhelming feeling that takes control over our emotions, thoughts, and actions. When we allow fear to settle in, we argue with the devil's plans and no longer operate under God's power. God is love, and no man can take it. Knowing who you are in Christ will play a major role in your new identity once you accept Christ as your Lord and Savior. The new identity comes from washing your sins through baptism and receiving the Holy Spirit. God's words say in **Matthew 3:16 AMP**

After Jesus was baptized, He came up immediately out of the water; and behold, the heavens were opened, and he (John) saw the Spirit of God descending as a dove and lighting on Him (Jesus).

When Jesus died on the cross and arose on the 3rd day, God left Jesus' Spirit with us called the Holy Ghost (Spirit). Through His Spirit, we can hear and communicate with God, get direction, get comfort, and get understanding/revelation. This is important to our salvation because this gives us the ability to fight the wiles of the devil. (**Read Ephesians 6:11**)

In this book, you will read personal experiences that I went through and or am going through. This is in no way to harm, talk about, or point blame toward anyone. The purpose behind telling personal information is to obey God so that the next person can be free. We all have trials and difficult situations that happen to us, and we must share them to help save another person. Our testimonies will help unlock somebody else's freedom.

Revelations 12:11 AMP

And they overcame and conquered him because of the blood of the Lamb and because of the word of their testimony, for they did not love their life and renounce their faith even when faced with death.

CHAPTER 1

The Kings of Israel

REVELATION 1:5-6 (NKJV)

⁵ and from Jesus Christ, the faithful witness, the firstborn from the dead, and the ruler over the kings of the earth. To Him who loved us and washed us from our sins in His own blood, ⁶ and has made us kings and priests to His God and Father, to Him [be] glory and dominion forever and ever. Amen.

To understand Jezebel, you must understand the history of the kings before Ahab. There were a few kings that were mentioned before King Ahab came about.

1 KINGS 15:25-27 (AMP)

²⁵ Now Nadab the son of Jeroboam began to reign over Israel in the second year of Asa king of Judah, and he reigned over Israel for two years. ²⁶ He did evil in the sight of the Lord and walked in the way of his father [Jeroboam] and in his sin [of idolatry], with which he made Israel sin. ²⁷ Baasha the son of Ahijah of the house (tribe) of Issachar conspired against Nadab, and Baasha struck him down at Gibbethon, which belonged to the Philistines, while Nadab and all Israel were laying siege to Gibbethon.

8

While reading this scripture, I noticed that King Nadab was evil in the sight of the Lord and he walked in the ways of his father. This indicates that his father, Jeroboam was also evil before the Lord. This is what's taking place in our world today. Kids, especially young boys/men, are walking in the footsteps of their fathers. When kids grow up, they watch their parents and try to mimic their parent's actions without even realizing it. You can observe how an adopted child and their biological parents share traits without them ever meeting. You will notice traits that they share. Some parents are in jail, and when their child grows up, they also get into jail. Why is that? The Bible mentions that we are to pray and ask for forgiveness for our forefather's sins and our sins. Some curses have been passed on to us because of the sins of the generation before us.

Leviticus 26:40-42 (AMP)

> [40] 'If they confess their wickedness and the wickedness of their forefathers, in their unfaithfulness which they have committed against Me and also in their acting with hostility toward Me [41] I also was acting with hostility toward them and brought them into the land of their enemies then if their uncircumcised (sin-filled) hearts are humbled and they accept the punishment for their wickedness, [42] then I will remember My covenant with Jacob, and also My covenant with Isaac, and also My covenant with Abraham, and remember the land.

The scripture says that we are to confess our wickedness and the wickedness of our forefathers. It also mentioned in the last verse that God will remember His covenant with

Abraham and remember the land. What that means is God will go back to the promise He made and will offer you forgiveness; One thing I want you to know is, even if a person receives forgiveness, that doesn't automatically remove the demons that they inherited. Let's take a look at that: There are generational curses that are passed through the bloodline. When those curses are not broken, the devil has legal access to you, your kids, your grandkids, and all the generations after them. Demons travel through the bloodline until the curse has been lifted and broken. For this to happen, a person has to go through deliverance/ curse breaking and the demon has to be removed from the person and or bloodline. Jesus' entire ministry was rebuking and casting out devils (demons). In today's time, many people are attending churches where deliverance isn't taking place and demons aren't mentioned. This is one of the reasons why people are staying bound and possessed by these evil spirits. Some churches are more worried about paying their church bill and monitoring church attendance rather than sharing and preaching the truth. We live in a society that says, "You don't ask; we don't tell." I think about it often because people have multiple personalities and mental disorders and so end up in the mental hospital. These people are demon-possessed and need to be freed from Satan and the curses that have been passed down to them and in some cases, the person opened themselves up to it without even realizing it. Someone in the family has to take a stand and say "NO" to Satan, not my family, and "not my kids!"

KING BAASHA

Baasha kills King Nadab and becomes king over Israel.

(1 KINGS 15: 28-30)

> [28] *So Baasha killed Nadab in the third year of Asa king of Judah, and reigned in his place.* [29] *As soon as he was king, Baasha struck down all the household of Jeroboam. He did not leave for Jeroboam anyone alive, but he destroyed them in accordance with the word of the LORD which He had spoken through His servant Ahijah the Shilonite* [30] *because of the sins committed by Jeroboam and which he made Israel commit, and because he provoked the LORD God of Israel to anger.*

God tells Jehu a prophecy against Bassha and says because of Bassha's evilness and how he caused God's people, the people of Israel to sin provoking God to anger with their sins of idol worship. God then says that He will sweep away Baasha and the entire household (family). To sweep (kill). God also says that for anyone who dies in the city, the dogs will eat them (**Read 1 Kings 16:1-4**).

KING ELAH

Now, Elah Baasha came to reign in his place. He became king over Israel in Tirzah and ruled for two years. Elah had a servant named Zimir, who was Elah's commander and chief over half his chariots. There came a time and day when Elah became drunk, and because of the curse placed over the family (from Baasha evil doings), Elah's servant Zimir struck Elah dead and reigned in his place. As soon as he became king, he also struck (killed) Elah's entire family. He didn't leave one man alive **(Read 1 Kings 16:11)**.

The prophecy given to Jehu was now fulfilled.

1 KINGS 16:3 (AMP)

For all the sins of Baasha and the sins of Elah his son, which they committed, and made Israel commit, provoking the Lord God of Israel to anger with their idols.

As you read this scripture, you will again see that Elah was also evil and that the curse had been passed down to him. Provoking God to anger leads to the death of the entire bloodline. We must repent of our sins and the sins before us. There are instances where God will lift the curse if one person repents. We will later read more about that later on.

King Zimir

1 Kings 16: 15-19 (AMP)

> [15] *In the twenty-seventh year of Asa king of Judah, Zimri reigned [over Israel] for seven days at Tirzah. Now the troops were camped against Gibbethon, [a city] which belonged to the Philistines,* [16] *and the people who were camped heard it said, "Zimri has conspired and has also struck down the king." So all Israel made Omri, the commander of the army, king over Israel that day in the camp.* [17] *Then Omri went up from Gibbethon, and all Israel with him.*

And Notice:

1. Each king so far has sinned in the sight of the Lord.
2. The punishment for those sins was death.
3. In the case of Zimri, he died by suicide.
4. Sin leads to destruction and then death.

What we have to realize is that sin leads to death. God isn't pleased when we break his commandments and fall into the same sins as our forefathers. Leaders are important because they can lead you to God or away from God. Being led away is being led away from your destiny and purpose in life. Many times today, people are dying prematurely and never fulfilling their God-given destiny. The best example that comes to mind is going out to eat, having dessert, and then leaving and never paying your bill. The check is now left open and now has to be voided out for the company to pay. When we leave this world without filling God's calling, we leave the check open for the next person to close. If it's a generational curse and you refuse to have it broken, the curse will go to the next available family member. Let's look at this from another perspective. Example: If you have a teaching gift and are supposed to minister to troubled kids. Now the kids suffer and have to wait for the next in line. In life, we have people that are connected to us and need everything that God has placed in us. Our gifts aren't for ourselves but for us to help someone that needs our gifts.

I recently learned;

(1). that what I go through will grow me. It's in the darkest times of our life when we seek after God more. When we have darkness all around us, God's light is right there next to us, shining in and becoming our flashlight. Flashlights give us just enough light to see what's ahead of us. I also learned

(2). our gifts are to be used to help someone. The things we go through in life we must learn from them and share them with others that are going through the same thing. We are to be a walking testimony for the Lord.

KING OMRI

1 KING 16:21-22

> ²¹ *Then the people of Israel were divided in half. Half of the people followed Tibni the son of Ginath, to make him king, and the other half followed Omri.* ²² *But the people who followed Omri prevailed over the people who followed Tibni the son of Ginath. So Tibni died and Omri became king.*

1 KING 16:25-26

> ²⁵ *But Omri did evil in the sight of the Lord, and acted more wickedly than all who came before him.* ²⁶ *He walked in all the ways of Jeroboam the son of Nebat and in his sin, which he made Israel commit, provoking the Lord God of Israel, [to anger] with their idols.*

Each time a new king was put in place, it was only a short time after that they became evil by worshiping other gods. A few patterns I see are:

1. God will remove and replace those that cause his people to stumble.

2. Causing God's kids to stumble has an expiration date and the ultimate punishment is death.

They were causing God's children to sin and anger the Lord, which caused Him to bring judgment. We don't want to anger the Lord to the point that there is no return. God gives us many chances to try again. However, time runs out.

CHAPTER 2

King Ahab & Queen Jezebel

Deuteronomy 32:39 (NLT)

Look now; I myself am he! There is no other god but me! I am the one who kills and gives life; I am the one who wounds and heals; no one can be rescued from my powerful hand!

When I think of Bonnie and Clyde, I think of Ahab and Jezebel. Ahab became king after King Omri. Omri was Ahab's father. Early on, when Ahab is introduced in **1 King 16:30** The writer mentions right away that he also did evil in the sight of the Lord. However, he was more evil than any other kings before him. What I noticed when reading this book was that, each king did not learn the lesson from the king before. They came in as kings and had their own agenda. Each king also angered God and did more evil than the king before. Each generation is worst off than the first.

Ahab, on the other hand, married Queen Jezebel which was against the Lord.

1 KING 16:31-33 (AMP)

> [31] It came about, as if it had been a trivial thing for Ahab to walk in the sins of Jeroboam the son of Nebat, that he married Jezebel the daughter of Ethbaal king of the Sidonians, and went and served Baal and worshiped him. [32] So he erected an altar for Baal in the house of Baal which he built in Samaria. [33] Ahab also made the Asherah. Ahab did more to provoke the Lord God of Israel than all the kings of Israel who were before him.

As soon as Ahab married Jezebel, he worshiped another god called Baal. Not only did he worship another god, but he built an altar for Baal. Jezebel had no relationship with God, and she planted seeds in Ahab and got him to turn away from his God to worship her god. I want to point out a few things in this scripture about Jezebel that the Holy Spirit revealed to me, and they are:

1. Splits up relationships.
2. Is an evil leader.
3. Comes with a plan already in mind.
4. Looks for a passive person to control.
5. Wants power.
6. Separates you from God.
7. Causes a person to worship other gods.

God tells us not to be unequally yoked

2 Corinthians 6:14 (AMP)

Do not be unequally bound together with unbelievers [do not make mismatched alliances with them, inconsistent with your faith]. For what partnership can righteousness have with lawlessness? Or what fellowship can light have with darkness?

Why do we think this is? When reading this scripture, God knows that this can separate us from him and cause us to serve other gods. Our God is a jealous God and he wants us to himself. He is the creator that created you for a purpose. When you open yourself up to relationships with people who don't have the same beliefs as you, you don't just open yourself up physically but also spiritually. You open yourself up to their demons. You will begin to notice a shift in how you feel about God and you will begin to question your faith. This isn't limited to just physical relationships (romantic) but also people that you call your close friends, ones you tell your deepest secrets to, and family that you grow up with. Yes, family! Reminder: God tells us that our brothers and sisters are those that are following his commandments (**Read Luke 8:21**).

BAAL

Baal is a Canaanite and Phoenician deity, and the son of the Chief god El. Baal took the shape of a bull and was connected with fertility. Babies were sacrificed to Baal as a form of worship. Baal was known for a few acts that God is against, but let's focus on human sacrifice and eating food sacrifice offered to the idols (**Read Revelation 2:14**).

Let's look at the start of the Israelites worshiping other gods. In Exodus 32, Moses leaves the Israelites he had just saved out of the hand of Pharaoh (in Egypt) and goes up to the mountain to have time with God for 40 days and 40 nights. Aaron, Moses' brother, was left in charge of the Israelites. The Israelites began complaining about the length of time Moses had been gone, and they wanted a god that they could go before and make a sacrifice to. So, the Israelites gathered with Aaron and told him they wanted him to provide a god for them to make sacrifices and to worship. Aaron told the Israelites to take off all the gold rings in the ears of their wives, sons, and daughters. Aaron then used an engraving tool and made the gold into a molten calf. Aaron then states that this calf was the god who took them out of Egypt. God was not pleased with what Aaron had done and God told Moses that he needed to return because of the Israelite were worshiping other gods, which was forbidden **(Read Exodus 32:1-6**).

In today's time, that is exactly what is happening. There have been times I have been looking for God in the midst of a trial, and there were moments when I didn't hear him. So I begin to allow fear and doubt to come into my mind. God's word tells us to cast down those thoughts immediately. If we allow those thoughts to sink in and we meditate on those thoughts, we will then believe the thoughts being released into our minds. The mind is indeed a battlefield.

When the Israelites no longer saw Moses, which was their way to hear from God, they began to panic instead of waiting on Moses to return. How many of us are guilty of not having enough patients or can't wait long enough to hear from God? Moses went to the mountain to have time with God and in his absence, Aaron was left in charge. Aaron allowed the people's complaining to manipulate his mind and he was trying to satisfy the people vs. satisfying God and his commandments. God's word says that obedience is better than sacrifice (**Read 1 Samuel 15:22**).

In doing so, they broke one important commandment, which was thou shall not worship any other gods (**Read Exodus 22:20 and Exodus 20:3**).

Our God is a jealous God and He makes that clear in (**Read Exodus 34:14**).

I want to leave you with this, anytime you act in rebellion to the instructions of God, you agree to the agenda of satan, and we are then operating under witchcraft.

1 SAMUEL 15:23 (AMP)

> *"For rebellion is as [serious as] the sin of divination (fortune-telling), And disobedience is as [serious as] false religion and idolatry. Because you have rejected the word of the LORD, He also has rejected [a]you as king."*

We have to stand on the promises of God and we have to be patient. I've learned that God doesn't move at my pace and His pace is not the same as our pace, His time is not the same as our time, and His victory isn't the same as our victory. If we say we trust God fully, then we must trust Him and His process.

CHAPTER 3

Worshiping of Other Gods

EXODUS 20:4-5 (NKJV)

[4] *"You shall not make for yourself a carved image--any likeness [of anything] that [is] in heaven above, or that [is] in the earth beneath, or that [is] in the water under the earth;* [5] *you shall not bow down to them nor serve them. For I, the LORD your God, [am] a jealous God, visiting the iniquity of the fathers upon the children to the third and fourth [generations] of those who hate Me.*

After reading the story about Aaron making a calf and how God was displeased is a great indication that we have to be careful about putting anything above God. Many of us today are so distracted by the things of this world that we don't even realize that God is not pleased with our behavior and the limitless time we spend outside of His word. We must be careful what we allow in our portals (eyes, ears, mouth, and mind). Listed below are a few gods that keep people from having a relationship with God.

TELEVISION -

People spend countless amounts of time watching movie after movie and show after show. Not knowing that with each new show or movie, they watch they are getting farther from God. Some people watch lustful, horror, murder, profanity, and magic/witchcraft movies and shows (to name a few) not knowing that they are planting seeds inside themselves.

Seeds of lust, fear, hate, and murder, They start having an interest in horoscopes, magic, spells, and seeing a witch for fortune telling. God tells us to stay away from those things.

Please review the 10 commandments at the end of this chapter.

Whatever you feed yourself daily will affect your life. Have you ever watched a scary movie and felt fear while watching it, jumping at every scene and then later going home and being afraid to go to sleep? I know I have. When I was 13 or 14, I remember being at my friends' house for the night. She turned on porn, and I remember feeling the urge to have sex while watching it. I didn't understand at the time what was happening to me and why I felt high urges for sex. Looking back at it now, this was a spiritual realm that I opened myself up to and didn't realize it. Later in high school/adult life, I faced molestation and rap (**to read more, please order my book My Journey To Salvation**). I was also sexually active at 13, which opened me up to soul ties. So many of our kids today are exposed to things we try to protect them from. It's important to have a conversation with your teenagers (if you have them) and explain this unseen world that is happening.

In today's time, we have to watch what we are viewing on TV and protect ourselves. If it doesn't line up with the word of God and or goes against the word of God, we have to question why you want to watch it. Ask God to reveal to you the things you shouldn't watch. Ask Him to place a conviction in your heart and ask Him for the strength to turn it off. If you have difficulty pulling away from the TV and sitting there for hours, TV has become more important to you than God. Turn it off and get back into worship with God.

MONEY-

1 TIMOTHY 6:10 (AMP)

> For the love of money [that is, the greedy desire for it
> and the willingness to gain it unethically] is a root
> of all sorts of evil, and some by longing for it have
> wandered away from the faith and pierced themselves
> [through and through] with many sorrows.

Relationships with family and friends have been broken because of money. There is an ex-friend of mine who is sitting in prison now for the rest of his life. He killed someone over drug money. This person they killed was also their best friend. Money is essential to living. We need money to buy groceries, rent, get gas, pay electric bills, etc. We have people robbing banks for money. They not only rob one bank but multiple. It's like they aren't satisfied. When we operate out of evil, we will never be satisfied. The Holy Spirit told me that evil intention leads to temporary satisfaction. The person may be happy at the moment but will eventually want more. More money, shoes, jewelry, clothes, electronics, boyfriends, girlfriends, cars, homes, etc.

HEBREW 13:5 (AMP)

> *Let your character [your moral essence, your inner nature] be free from the love of money [shun greed— be financially ethical], being content with what you have; for He has said, "I will never [under any circumstances] desert you [nor give you up nor leave you without support, nor will I in any degree leave you helpless], nor will I forsake or let you down or relax My hold on you [assuredly not]!"*

Remember, God wants us to be content with what we have. As you continue to read, you will see and understand how Jezebel is behind these evil desires.

MUSIC-

Music is one of the biggest keys to our hearts. God loves for us to come into His presence with praise and worship. It opens us up to hear and receive from God. Lucifer (Satan) was the worshiper in Heaven. He had a beautiful voice. Because of Satan's disobedience, he was kicked out of Heaven and thrown to the earth. He was thrown to earth for a length of time. He has been given authority over those who open themselves up to him.

When we choose to be disobedient, we agree with Satan. Satan likes to attack leaders because they are the foundation that holds Gods people together. He wants to distract any high-position leader that has fellowship and a relationship with God. He likes to put doubt into the leaders, especially the worship leaders.

When we worship God, Satan hates it. We are a constant reminder of why Satan was made and a of his fall from heaven. In case you don't know why Satan was made, he was made to worship God with praise and worship. He was the most beautiful angel created and had lots of diamonds and Jews. Satan began to envy God and wanted to be like Him. He wanted to have a throne that was higher than God. Satan not only deceived his own heart, but he took a 3rd of the angles with him. They were all kicked out of heaven and Satan fell like lightning to earth (**Read Isaiah 14:12-17**).

Listening to secular music opens you up to demons. The music played by these secular artists is inspired by the devil. Just like praise and worship, songs are inspired by God. The spiritual world is being opened and you will feel the presence of what you listened to. Emotions are given when music is played. Have you ever noticed how praise and worship set the atmosphere before church starts and how you can feel the presence of the Holy Spirit? It's the same as feeling the wind even though you can't see it. You feel the gentle breeze and it feels good. Music brings Heaven to earth. It puts us in a position to go before God and creates the space for variability. The same thing happens when you listen to secular music. It opens you to the demonic side and creates space for the enemy to attack you in every area of your life.

A lot of believers believe that they can listen to what they want and still please God. However, God wants all of us, not just some of us.

PEOPLE -

Have you ever been influenced by someone that you ignore the voice of the Holy Spirit to follow and or worship another person? God tells us not to put any other gods before Him, including people. When I was in a previous relationship, I allowed myself to be so distracted by him. I feared what he thought about me and how he would react to what I did. I would please this guy so he wouldn't be angry with me. I knew I would face the silent treatment if I didn't do what he said. This type of silent treatment would last days and even weeks. I felt myself walking on my tippy toes, trying not to make him mad—the type of fear that I was supposed to have in God I had in man. God tells us not to fear man but to fear God, who can destroy your soul and body (**Read Matthew 10:28**).

Can you imagine having the silent treatment from God or having God mad at you? You would feel empty and defeated.

People pleasing will cause you to disobey God's words and the prompting of the Holy Spirit.

Psalm 118:8 (AMP)

It is better to take refuge in the Lord Than to trust in man.

God tells us to take safety in the Lord and not trust "man." Depending on your background and how a person is raised, they may look for love in people rather than love from God. If a girl/woman had no father figure, they might look for love in a boy/man. This young lady may lose her virginity at an early age and have several sexual partners before she turns 18. She may also feel rejected and have trouble having a healthy relationship with men. This type of person sets little to no standards and tries to please people (especially men). If you're dealing with a boy who grows up without a father figure, he may not know who he is as a person. This person also grows up feeling rejected and can depend on people vs. God. They often look for approval from men and in most cases, they get into trouble with the law because they find approval from the streets. A small number turn out ok, but they still deal with rejection. This can be in the form of being unable to show love, not knowing how to be a father, not knowing who they are as a man, and inability to trust and have a healthy relationship. The person may operate normally, but deep inside, they are dealing with rejections.

This issue of pleasing people starts in the home. When a healthy relationship base is set at home, you will have a higher chance of having a healthy start in life. Our goal should be to make God happy with what we are doing. We should be more concerned about what God thinks about us and less about what man thinks. Today I strive to please God and obey what He is telling me. Allow God to be the father to the fatherless and a provider to the needy. Some people may need love and acceptance. God can be both of those for you. Just accept him and watch what He can do.

QUESTIONS TO ASK YOURSELF

1. Who are you putting before God?
2. Who has God told you to let go?
3. Who has more influence over you than God?
4. Do you fear God more than man?
5. Do you have any idols that you need to destroy?
6. Are there any movies or music you need to stop engaging in?

IDOLS -

EXODUS 32 1-6 (AMP)

> ¹ *Now when the people saw that Moses delayed coming down from the mountain, they gathered together before Aaron and said to him, "Come, make us a [a] god who will go before us; as for this Moses, the man who brought us up from the land of Egypt, we do not know what has become of him."* ² *So Aaron replied to them, "Take off the gold rings that are in the ears of your wives, your sons and daughters, and bring them to me."* ³ *So all the people took off the gold rings that were in their ears and brought them to Aaron.* ⁴ *And he took the gold from their hands, and fashioned it with an engraving tool and made it into a molten [b]calf; and they said, "This is your god, O Israel, who brought you up from the land of Egypt."* ⁵ *Now when Aaron saw the molten calf, he built an altar before it; and Aaron made a proclamation, and said, "Tomorrow shall be a feast to the Lord!"* ⁶ *So they got up early the next day and offered burnt offerings, and brought peace offerings; then the people sat down to eat and drink, and got up to play [shamefully—without moral restraint].*

Who have you idolized and placed over God? I remember coming to Christ and trying to trust God and hear from him. I wanted to see God and hear from him the same way I heard and saw from people. I didn't understand that you could only hear Him through the Spirit and the small still voice. I would reach out to people for answers because I was impatient. We live in a society where people want things now and they don't want to wait on them. That was me a few years ago. It reminds me of the Israelite a lot. They were getting impatient because Moses was on the mountain with God. They didn't want to wait on Moses' return as instructed. In the waiting period, Aaron yielded to the people's request and made a false god before the people.

This type of worship made God angry and He was ready to destroy the Israelites. Instead of destroying the people, God sent Moses back down the hill and Moses destroyed the altar that was built in place of God. Moses melted the calf and made the people drink it (**Read Exodus 32**)

Please read the following scripture on what the Bible says about worshiping idols.

1. Leviticus 26:1 (AMP)

"You shall not make idols for yourselves, nor shall you erect an image, a sacred pillar or an obelisk, nor shall you place any figured stone in your land so that you may bow down to it; for I am the Lord your God.

2. Ezekiel 36:18 (AMP)

So I poured out My wrath on them for the blood which they had shed on the land and because they had defiled it with their idols.

3. Jeremiah 1:16 (AMP)

I will speak My judgments against them for all the wickedness of those who have abandoned (rejected) Me, offered sacrifices or burned incense to other gods, and worshiped the [idolatrous] works of their own hands.

4. 2 Kings 17:12 (AMP)

*And they served idols, of which the Lord had said to them,
"You shall not do this thing."*

5. Ezekiel 20:8 (AMP)

*But they rebelled against Me and were not willing to listen to
Me; they did not throw away the detestable things on which
they feasted their eyes, nor did they give up the idols of Egypt.
"Then I decided to pour out My wrath on them and finish My
anger against them in the land of Egypt.*

God's scriptures clearly state how He feels if we worship any other god besides Him. The Bible also mentions that our God is a jealous God (**Read Deuteronomy 4:24**).

This reminds me of being in a relationship with somebody and then stepping outside the relationship. The natural reaction will be anger, jealousy, betrayal, hurt, and confusion. This is how God feels when we step outside the relationship boundaries that He has given us (His word). It causes you to be separated from God until you ask for repentance. God mentions that we will also reap what we sow. Just because we ask for forgiveness doesn't mean we won't reap the punishment the sin brought.

There are so many things that can take our focus off of God. Going through different trials and tribulations will help you lean on God more and help you stay away from idols. I learned to let go of all my idols through the most difficult situation that happened in my life.

Listed below are a few more idols that God placed on my heart to mention. These are a few and I'm sure there are more.

1. Alcoholism
2. Porn
3. Masturbation
4. Smoking
5. Stealing
6. Shopping
7. Pills (sleeping pills)
8. Food
9. People
10. Music
11. Movies
12. Video Games
13. Social Media
14. Self Harm

These are all used to cope with life and to relieve the pain that an individual is feeling. The more I turned to God, the more He freed me from the addictions that I faced. Addiction is another word for "idol." Indulging in a negative behavior takes away the pain that only lasts temporarily. However, engaging in God and His word is a feeling that lasts forever and it takes away the pain completely. People turn to these addictions to get away from the pain or negative emotions that they feel. I'm here to tell you that JESUS is the answer. If He healed me, then He can heal you too. Healing means trusting in God and leaning on Him in your most difficult and painful situations. The process may be slow, but the healing is everlasting.

1 KINGS 16:29-34 (AMP)

> [29] *Ahab the son of Omri became king over Israel in the thirty-eighth year of Asa king of Judah, and Ahab the son of Omri reigned over Israel in Samaria for twenty-two years.* [30] *Ahab the son of Omri did evil in the sight of the Lord more than all [the kings] who were before him.* [31] *It came about, as if it had been a trivial thing for Ahab to walk in the sins of Jeroboam the son of Nebat, that he married [a]Jezebel the daughter of Ethbaal king of the Sidonians, and went and served Baal and worshiped him.* [32] *So he erected an altar for Baal in the house of Baal which he built in Samaria.* [33] *Ahab also made the Asherah. Ahab did more to provoke the Lord God of Israel than all the kings of Israel who were before him.* [34] *In his days, Hiel the Bethelite rebuilt Jericho. He laid its foundations with the loss of Abiram his firstborn, and set up its gates with the loss of his youngest son Segub, in accordance with the word of the Lord, which He spoke through Joshua the son of Nun.*

Here are a few things to remember about the spirit of Jezebel and what happens when you worship other idols.

1. Jezebel causes you to start relationships that are not of God.

Ahab started a relationship with Jezebel that shouldn't have taken place. In doing so, Ahab became a slave to what Jezebel wanted. Even though he was king, Jezebel manipulated and controlled Ahab. God tells us not to be unequally yoked. Accepting relationships that draw you away from God will lead you to ultimate destruction.

I remember when I entered into two relationships from my past. I had family members and friends telling me not to leave my home state for this person and not to enter into these relationships. However, I didn't listen and entered these relationships despite the warnings. Slowly I began to fade away from who I was and became the person my abusers wanted. I was too afraid to speak up for myself. I held on to these relationships that I knew weren't good for me. These relationships destroyed my health mentally, physically, and emotionally. Being in this type of relationship will tear you apart.

2. Jezebel causes you to worship other idols.

Once King Ahab married Jezebel, he began to worship Baal. Even though he knew God forbade this. I remember being introduced to weed, clubs, drinking, strip clubs, cussing, porn, and masturbation from a past relationship. These were things that I wasn't doing before but I slowly got introduced to them. Over time I was becoming the person they wanted vs. the person God had called me to be. I completely turned my back on God and was living a dangerous life leading me to eternal hell.

3. Jezebel causes a division between you and God.

The moment you walk away from God is the moment you will feel the separation from God, and you will no longer feel guilty for doing wrong. You will no longer think of the consequences of your actions. It's like playing russian roulette, hoping the next round isn't the bullet that will take your life. I remember living without fear of eternal life. Looking back, I am thankful I never reached the bullet that could have ended my life.

4. Worshiping other idols causes you to do evil.

Anytime we open ourselves up to other gods, we do things outside God's will. Some people kill people and or plot to kill. After reading the story of King Ahab and Jezebel, I found out that Jezebel plotted to kill the prophets of God, and she also plotted and succeeded in having Naboth Killed.

One experience that happened to me was I was given a plate of food by an ex and thinking nothing of it; I ate it. I became sick that same day and had flu-like symptoms. Little did I know this person had poisoned my food. Years later, I learned through the Holy Spirit while at church. The pastor mentioned that some of you should be dead and that people tried to kill you. He said the devil was scratching his head trying to figure out how that person made it. At that moment, the plate of food that was given to me came to mind. I thought to myself Oh my (I said the person's name) tried to kill me.

5. Worshiping other idols will cause you to degrade yourself and compromise.

In my experience, I worshiped relationships with people. I became insecure about who I was and what I wanted. I no longer knew what I wanted and only did what the person wanted me to do. One of my exes told me that I was easy to manipulate. I remember this as if it was yesterday. I was at the mall, shopping for some new clothes for a job I was about to start. I had a few shirts that looked the same but different colors and he said, why are you getting the same shirt in different colors? Without thinking, I said I put some back. He immediately said you are so easy to manipulate. I didn't think about those words he said to me until later on (years). I learned not to feel how I should feel while I was in this relationship. I learned that my feelings didn't matter. I was so stressed and depressed from this relationship that I was 125 lbs. I barely ate because I feared what the person would say to me when I ate. I remember tip-toeing to the pantry to get a snack and hearing him tell me I shouldn't be eating that late. I no longer knew what it was like to be myself. Later on in life had to figure out who I was all over again. I didn't realize that I was dealing with a person who had the spirit of Jezebel.

6. Worshiping other idols causes you to hate who God created.

When we step outside of Gods will for our life we step outside his covering. It's like we are saying I got it, God, step back and watch me work. I began to hate myself and question why God created me and my purpose. I didn't want to live. I hated life and everything that came with it. I didn't realize that what I was going through came because I disobeyed Him.

LEVITICUS 26:18 (AMP)

If in spite of all this you still will not listen to Me and be obedient, then I will punish you seven times more for your sins.

When we are disobedient to God's word, we open the doors to satan to cause destruction to our lives. We give the devil a foothold to us, our kids, and generations to come. The good news is that we can ask for forgiveness and break generational curses and turn from that sin. When Jesus came, He came to set the captives free.

7. Worshiping idols can and will split families apart.

This topic hits home in multiple places for me. Interactions with this spirit will draw a line between you and your family. Isolation is a big factor for a person caring about this spirit. Early on in a previous relationship, I was in I was being stripped away from my family. I didn't realize what was happening. I just noticed that I spoke to my family less often and had little desire to go home. Manipulation words and division were given and I slowly took the bait that my family wasn't close like my ex. I felt my family didn't support me as his family supported me. My past was often brought up and I believed the lies being told. Those lies became my reality. Years after leaving this person, they began to do the same thing to my kids. He manipulated them to leave, making them feel like he had more to offer them. This spirit has no emotions, and it plays off your emotions. This is a spirit that you have to stand firm on, or it will devour you.

1 PETER 5:8 (AMP)

Be sober [well balanced and self-disciplined], be alert and cautious at all times. That enemy of yours, the devil, prowls around like a roaring lion [fiercely hungry], seeking someone to devour.

God says to be sober and alert at **ALL TIMES**. Are you ready to be a soldier for the Lord and be on guard at all times?

WAYS TO BE ALERT:

1. Pray and ask God for the Spirit of discernment.
2. Fasting.
3. Remember scripture.
4. Be obedient.
5. Study God's word.
6. Listen to the Holy Spirit.
7. Be watchful.

THE 10 COMMANDMENTS (READ EXODUS 20:2-17)

1. You shall have no other gods before Me.
2. You shall not make idols.
3. You shall not take the name of the Lord your God in vain.
4. Remember the Sabbath day, to keep it holy.
5. Honor your father and your mother.
6. You shall not murder.
7. You shall not commit adultery.
8. You shall not steal.
9. You shall not bear false witness against your neighbor.
10. You shall not covet.

CHAPTER 4

Prophets of Baal Defeated

ROMANS 12:19-21 (NLT)

[19] Dear friends, never take revenge. Leave that to the righteous anger of God. For the Scriptures say, "I will take revenge; I will pay them back," says the LORD. [20] Instead, "If your enemies are hungry, feed them. If they are thirsty, give them something to drink. In doing this, you will heap burning coals of shame on their heads." [21] Don't let evil conquer you, but conquer evil by doing good.

C an you think of a time when you were defeated? Can you remember the emotions you felt? Living the life I lived and dealing with people from my past sometimes puts me in situations where I've felt defeated and I felt victory. You will face obstacles when you are a child of God walking according to His word. God allows these trials to happen for a few reasons.

1. Builds your faith.

2. Causes you to grow in an area you are weak.

3. It forces you to pray more.

4. It forces you to fast more.

5. In some cases, causes you to love your enemies more.

6. It forces you to see what areas you still struggle with in life.

7. Builds your character.

8. It makes you look more like Christ.

I see trails as a self-reflection. When I first got divorced, I had a lot of hurt, pain, and anger that was built up inside me. I wanted to do whatever I could to make the person feel as bad as I felt. If they said something to me, I would fuss/cuss back. It was like evil for evil; you step on my shoe, I step on yours, you cuss me out, then I'll cuss you out. It was a never-ending cycle. The truth is two people were hurting and instead of being mature adults, we did what we were taught and all we knew. Which is to get even. Nobody taught me how to pray when I have troubles, or to fast when you're dealing with demons, and talk to God instead of gossiping. Instead, I allowed my emotions to carry me minute by minute, hour by hour, and day by day. Unfortunately, this is how many people are fighting their battles. The Bible says in Ephesians 6 that we wrestle not against flesh and blood but against the principalities (**Read Ephesians 6:10-12**)

As the years passed, I began to feel convicted for talking and behaving out of God's character. I chose to do better and to become more of what God wanted and less of what I wanted. I was seeking God more; I sought spiritual counseling and spiritual deliverance. I began to ignore the remarks and harsh behaviors of my ex. I started to pray for him and started to see past the flesh and saw more into the spiritual. I still had emotions and wounds that needed to heal, but because I saw what I was going through as a spiritual attack, it was easier to deal with. I did have times when I acted out of my flesh. However, it was a learning experience to retrain my brain from what I was used to, to what I was becoming. One prominent emotion that lingered in me was fear and anxiety.

No matter how many counseling sessions I went through, how many scriptures I read, how much I prayed and hat feeling never left. I battled with fear taking over me without warning. I didn't want to feel the fear, but I couldn't control it. I will later talk about this fear and how I finally became free in a later chapter.

As I studied and read about the Prophet Elijah, I thought, what a brave man. Elijah faced some hard times as well. But in his trials, God was with him. Elijah faced victory and fear. He also ran from Jezebel in fear for his life. Below you will read how Jezebel was mad that her prophets were killed, so she put a hit out for Elijah's life. Let's read the story of Elijah's victory.

1 KINGS 18:25-29 (AMP)

[25] Elijah said to the prophets of Baal, "Choose one bull for yourselves and prepare it first, since there are many of you; and call on the name of your god, but put no fire under it." [26] So they took the bull that was given to them and prepared it, and called on the name of Baal from morning until noon, saying, "O Baal, hear and answer us." But there was no voice and no one answered. And they leaped about the altar which they had made. [27] At noon Elijah mocked them, saying, "Cry out with a loud voice, for he is a god; either he is occupied, or he is out [at the moment], or he is on a journey. Perhaps he is asleep and must be awakened!" [28] So they cried out with a loud voice [to get Baal's attention] and cut themselves with swords and lances in accordance with their custom, until the blood flowed out on them. [29] As midday passed, they played the part of prophets and raved dramatically until the time for offering the evening sacrifice; but there was no voice, no one answered, and no one paid attention.

> [30] *Then Elijah said to all the people, "Come near to me." So all the people approached him. And he repaired and rebuilt the [old] altar of the Lord that had been torn down [by Jezebel].* [31] *Then Elijah took twelve stones in accordance with the number of the tribes of the sons of Jacob, to whom the word of the Lord had come, saying, "Israel shall be your name."* [32] *So with the stones Elijah built an altar in the name of the Lord. He made a trench around the altar large enough to hold [d]two measures of seed.* [33] *Then he laid out the wood and cut the ox in pieces and laid it on the wood.* [34] *And he said, "Fill four pitchers with water and pour it on the burnt offering and the wood." And he said, "Do it the second time." And they did it the second time. And he said, "Do it the third time." And they did it a third time.* [35] *The water flowed around the altar, and he also filled the trench with water.*

There are a few things that I must point out.

1. Jezebel sent prophets out to do her work.

Who has been sent out against you? Who is monitoring your life? One thing I know about this spirit is that the spirit of Jezebel doesn't works alone. This spirit has other spirits to do the dirty work. Dealing with this spirit myself, multiple people have attacked me because of one individual. This spirit will use your kids against you, family, friends, and coworkers, and you will also go to great lengths and contact your church. This spirit will stop at nothing to destroy you.

2. Jezebel's spirit promotes the cutting of the flesh (Baal worship).

The Bible mentioned that her prophets walked around their altar, cutting themself so that Baal would answer them. Baal never came and the people bled out. This is a form of self-harm.

Today, we see and hear cases of people harming themselves. In some cases, people are dying because of suicide. There is one lady I knew that had many knife cuts on her arm. She mentioned that she cut herself to get rid of the pain that she was feeling. This is a demonic act to do. People who self-harm need deliverance.

3. Jezebel caused her prophets to worship a false god.

This is the deception of the enemy. So many people are deceived today. They believe that they are hearing from God and they are not. There is one young lady I know who believes that God is harming/torturing her here on earth. The truth is she's opened the door to the enemy and Satan had a legal case built against her. She explained the torments she faced and the thoughts that she had. I could see the torments she faced by her actions. One night I encountered a dream where I was in a dark place. It looked like a huge underground basement. People were all around. I was standing off to the side and I remembered a lady standing before Satan. He was about to cast her into the pit, but she began crying and crying and reminding him of everything she had done in his name. There were two demons that I can recall that stood one on each side of Satan. I remember waking up and feeling in my spirit deception. This lady thought she was doing good, but

Satan deceived her and now she was going to hell. That is many people today. Some believers believe that once saved is always saved, But Peter teaches us that we have to deny ourselves daily, which means we have to strive to be free from sin daily. God tells us to flee from sin. "Flee" means to run from it and not look back.

Do you remember the story of Lot's wife in the Bible? God was saving Lot and his family from Sodom and Gomorrah's destruction. Lot's wife looked back and was turned into a pillar of salt. When God removes you from a situation that is destroying you, He doesn't want you to return to it.

4. In the end, God will win.

At the beginning of the scripture, it mentioned in verse 25 that there were many Baal prophets. Elijah was outnumbered by what he could see in the physical realm, but because of his faith, he knew that there was more with him than what was with them. God's word says to fix our eyes on unseen things (**Read 2 Corinthians 4:18**).

There have been times in my personal life when I allowed myself to focus on what I saw and felt. It causes you to have fear and to doubt God's word. I remember early on in my Christian walk, I would give God my situation and then take it back because of what I saw. It didn't look like God was moving fast enough. Looking back on that, I didn't trust God or have enough faith. I allowed the overwhelming feeling and pressure of the situation to put matters back in my hands, which didn't get me anywhere. Many times, my battles were won, and God gave me grace and victory. I felt myself getting a step closer to God. Then something would

47

happen with one of my court cases, and I would fall back ten steps from God. I was playing tug-a-war with God. Unfortunately, this lasted for years. I finally reached a point where I didn't want to play this game anymore. I finally dropped the rope and said God, I give my case to you, I give my kids to you, and I give all of my problems to you. I must say the heat turned up and a particular person was attacking me and my kids were being used as bullets. My kids were manipulated to turn against me and to run away from me, there were false accusations made about me, and there were false accusations against my husband as well. No matter how much evidence I could show in court, it was dismissed, or it was acknowledged and the opposite party was "talked to" and the orders were reinforced. I'm saying all of this for a few reasons.

- When you decide to walk with God, you will face the same persecutions that Jesus faced. God tells us to count it all joy. (**Read James 1:2**)

- When you choose God you are choosing to go into battle with the enemy. The enemy will use people that are close to you to attack you. He will use those you love to hurt and betray you, just like Judas did to Jesus.

- Going through trials and tribulations will strengthen your faith and teach you how to fight in the spiritual realm.

- Remember that your battle starts in the spiritual realm before it starts in the physical. So you must start your battle in the spiritual, not with people in the flesh.

- It doesn't matter what your situation looks like but remember what God's word says. There is a scripture for every situation that you face. So, stay faithful to God's word.

- Your enemy is not with people but with the spiritual wickedness in high places. Satan has already lost the battle, so your victory is already here. Rejoice in it! HALLELUJAH!

- When you genuinely give your problems to God, you can finally have peace and victory.

- Just because you don't see things happening physically doesn't mean that nothing is happening spiritually. Don't allow your eyes and emotions to control you. Seek God always!

I want to leave you with this. There was an incident that took place in my life in 2022. This incident tried to break me as a person, mother, and daughter of God. I remember not wanting to get out of bed, and I felt the spirit of depression trying to enter me. It was a Sunday morning, and I was lying in bed, and I told myself I had to get up and go to church. I had to practice what I preached (I'm a pastor). I gathered all the strength I had in me, and I went to church. Everyone around me knew something was wrong, but I didn't care. I knew I was where I needed to be. I was in the spiritual hospital. I sat through the first service feeling heavy and more depressed. I also felt like I didn't want to be there. I was there at church, but my mind was someplace else. I honestly can't remember one word that was taught. I then gathered myself together for the second service. When the praise and worship came on, it was between God and me. I poured my eyes out to God. I was on the floor crying and weeping, and at that moment, I felt depression lift off me; I felt the strength to get up and to keep fighting. I sat through that sermon, and the message was right on time. I later had the spirit of God overtake me, and I began to prophesy to multiple people. Since then, I have been on fire for God. What I noticed in this walk with God is He will use you at your lowest point in life. God's word tells us when we are weak we are made strong. The strength comes from God.

The devil wants to keep God's people surrounded with depression and worry. If he can get us in our emotions, then he can stop us from operating in the gifts God had stored in us. Gifts that cannot be taken back and gifts that we were born with. It doesn't matter where you've been, what you've done, or how far you walked away. You can always come back to God and repent and turn your life over to God.

Never despise where you currently are with God. There is a purpose to what you are going through. As I write this book, I now know I had to go through it to share my experience. My experience will set others free from the hands of Jezebel..

DO'S AND DON'T WITH JEZEBEL

1. Let your no be no and your yes be yes.
2. Don't allow this spirit to manipulate you.
3. Don't allow this spirit to control you.
4. Don't share information with this spirit (it will monitor your every move).
5. Don't express your emotions with a person that is carrying this spirit.
6. Don't share personal information with a person with this spirit (they will use the information against you).

7. Stand firm when dealing with this spirit.

8. Don't cater or over-explain to a person with this spirit.

9. Don't allow them to have the upper hand over you.

10. Be alert when dealing with a person with this spirit.

11. Be calm.

12. Be consistent in your "Don't".

13. Don't put your guard down.

14. Don't come into an agreement with this spirit.

NOTES

CHAPTER 5

Elijah Runs From Jezebel

ISAIAH 41:10-12 (NLT

[10] Don't be afraid, for I am with you. Don't be discouraged, for I am your God. I will strengthen you and help you. I will hold you up with my victorious right hand. [11] "See, all your angry enemies lie there, confused and humiliated. Anyone who opposes you will die and come to nothing. [12] You will look in vain for those who tried to conquer you. Those who attack you will come to nothing.

How many times have you ran from a situation because of fear? Fear can come from fear of the unknown, people's thoughts, and not being in control of a situation. Even if you have victory in a particular area of your life, you may have fear because you don't know how it will work out. Having to face fear and get over it comes through trusting God. But what happens when you trust God, and it's still present in your life? I remember asking myself this same question. I prayed to God and asked him to reveal what I was doing and help me overcome this feeling that was eating at me. I spoke to many pastors about this, and they all said to give it to God. What I would think is I have given it to God. Fear would overcome me without my knowledge. I could sit at work not thinking about anything but work, and fear would come over me. There have been times when I may have to be in the same area as my abuser, who abused me sexually, mentally, and emotionally, and fear would overtake me without me thinking about it. My body was already putting up a defense because my mind recognized this individual (my ex) as a danger. Anytime I had to be in the presence of my ex, the fear would overtake me hours before. It was the type of fear that would last leading up to the event and throughout the interaction. This type of fear I felt was like I was on a roller coaster and as it is going up preparing to make that drop you get that intense fear before the drop. That's what I would feel.

Side Note: I also drank a lot of coffee which increases anxiety and makes you jittery. I later found out that people who have anxiety and fear should limit their caffeine intake.

I found myself going to great lengths to stay clear of him. I was running away just like Elijah did. The spirit of Jezebel is powerful. For most people who haven't heard of the Jezebel spirit, it's exactly what a narcissist is. The world views it as a narcissist, but for the book, we will discuss it for what it is 'Jezebel". Let's elaborate on what happened with Elijah when he ran from Jezebel.

3 Types of defense mechanism

1. **Flight-** If your body believes you can't overcome the danger but can avoid it by running, you will respond in a flight mode.

2. **Freeze-** This cause response will cause you to not move. Your mind is telling you to respond but the fear overtakes you and you don't move.

3. **Fight-** If your body tells you you're in danger and you feel that you can overpower the threat you respond in a fight mode.

1 KINGS 19:1-8 1

¹ *Now Ahab told Jezebel all that Elijah had done, and how he had killed all the prophets [of Baal] with the sword.* ² *Then Jezebel sent a messenger to Elijah, saying, "So may the gods do to me, and even more, if by this time tomorrow I do not make your [a]life like the life of one of them."* ³ *And Elijah was afraid and arose and ran for his life, and he came to [b]Beersheba which belongs to Judah, and he left his servant there.* ⁴ *But he himself traveled a day's journey into the wilderness, and he came and sat down under a juniper tree and asked [God] that he might die. He said, "It is enough; now, O Lord, take my life, for I am no better than my fathers."* ⁵ *He lay down and slept under the juniper tree, and behold, an angel touched him and said to him, "Get up and eat."* ⁶ *He looked, and by his head there was a bread cake baked on hot coal, and a pitcher of water. So he ate and drank and lay down again.* ⁷ *Then the angel of the Lord came again a second time and touched him and said, "Get up, and eat, for the journey is too long for you [without adequate sustenance]."* ⁸ *So he got up and ate and drank, and with the strength of that food he traveled forty days and nights to Horeb (Sinai), the mountain of God.*

HERE ARE SEVERAL CHARACTERISTICS OF THIS SPIRIT:

1. The spirit of Jezebel doesn't like to be defeated and or confronted.

Dealing with this spirit and co-parenting with someone who needs deliverance from this spirit can be very challenging. When this spirit has taken over a person's body, this person is no longer functioning from wisdom and is functioning and operating out of a demonic entity. Anytime you win a victory over a person with this spirit, you will feel their wrath. They will repay you through your relationship with people, family, kids, spouse, ministry, job, personal life, and health. Their mission is to destroy you and make you pay for hurting them.

2. This Jezebel spirit promotes fear in their victims.

As we read in **1 Kings 19:12** that she sent a messenger to Elijah that she wanted him dead just like her prophets were killed. She even took it a step further and said "let it be done to her what was done to them (false prophets) if Elijah wasn't killed by this time tomorrow". Little did she know she was setting a trap for herself. I remember when I had to go to court and the court findings went in my favor and they showed great anger after court. They used my kids against me, they attacked me with words, slandered my character, and they wouldn't follow the court's order. I found myself in court every other month until I gave this issue over to God. I want to tell you if you don't give the situation to God you will not win the battle. Jezebel is not a spirit you want to fight in the natural realm.

3. Jezebel overplays her hand because of pride.

Because these people have so much pride, they will overplay their hand, giving you many victories. This is also a hypocritical person. They never accept blame, and they blame everyone else for their actions. Even if they were caught in the wrong. As we will later read, Jezebel, was defeated, and she was the cause of her death. She said, "Let it be done to me what was done to them."

1 KING 19:2

Then Jezebel sent a messenger to Elijah, saying, "So may the gods do to me, and even more, if by this time tomorrow I do not make your [a]life like the life of one of them."

She spoke of her death.

4. Where there is a Jezebel, an Ahab is not far away.

In today's time, people with this spirit have to be liked by people. They gain energy from people to gain leverage and access to high positions. They are undercover and can hide this evil behavior from people. Only the victim and those close by know the truth. Once this person has an explosion (which they will), they will stay away from those who know who they are. People are normally surprised by their behavior because they are overly friendly people; they usually volunteer for any and everything. If you have kids with this person, they will volunteer at the kid's schools and seem like the parent of the year. Ahab can be anyone who will be submissive to the objective of the person with this Jezebel spirit.

Elijah had to have a season to regain his strength. He ran from Jezebel, and in the state he was in, God had to restore him. Dealing with this spirit will drain you physically, spiritually, mentally, and emotionally. This spirit has no emotions, so their attacks can be very intense. In my experience, they are very well-spoken people before the courts. (**Read 1 King 19:3**)

I remember asking God why I felt my emotions when dealing with this person in court and feeling like I couldn't get my answers out correctly. God answered me and said because you have emotions, and you are normal. It made sense once the Holy Spirit spoke those words to me. People that carry this spirit have lost their feelings and emotions. Because they take on the feelings and emotions of the demon/s. Maybe something happened to them in their past where they were taken advantage of, or maybe this was a generational curse passed to the next available vessel. The one thing I noticed is that these types of people say one thing and do another.

For example:

Let's say you're in a relationship with this person, and they say I don't like the way sundresses look, they look cheap, and I don't want you to wear them. Then days and weeks go past, and you overhear them giving another woman a compliment in a sundress. He's telling her the dress looks good on her and that he likes the dress. Later that day, you address the issue, and he pretends to be lost in words as to ever saying that, or they say well, sundresses don't look good on you. This is called gaslighting. There are many other ways they will gaslight you. Gaslighting is shifting blame and making you out to be the bad person. Even though all the evidence is pointing to them.

NOTICE THE PATTERNS

When dealing with this spirit in people, you will notice different seasons between peace and intensity. I know for a while, I didn't recognize the patterns. My husband had to say, "Do you see that this time of year, every year, he's attacking you or taking you to court." I had to ask myself what happened during this season. This person was attacking me. I later discovered it was this time that I filed for divorce, and it was another season that the divorce was finalized. Once I noticed that the person was suffering from rejection and other emotions that God revealed to me, it was easier to get through these seasons. I started to pray for him in the area God had revealed to me. Once I started to pray for this person healing, the attacks got worse, and I was tested more. I had to rely on God and not on what my problem looked like. I had to get counsel from the pastors just like Elijah had to be fed by the angel. I had to receive prayer to regain strength from the spiritual attacks, just like Elijah had to be fed food for the journey to come. I wasn't only being attacked in the physical realm but in my sleep. I had witches and snakes come and attack me. The battle was intense, but God was right there with me. Through these battles, I learned that a demonic world was right before my eyes.

WHEN YOU ARE IN THIS BATTLE, REMEMBER:

1. Don't give up **(Read 2 Chronicles 15:7)**.

2. Continue to pray **(Read 1 Thessalonians 5:17)**.

3. Press into God more than ever **(Read Proverbs 3:5-6)**.

4. Know that this battle belongs to the Lord **(Read Exodus 14:14)**.

5. Know that your battles are won through God and not from self **(Read Deuteronomy 20:4).**

If you are dreaming of snakes, please understand that God could be warning you that you have an enemy nearby.

NOTES

CHAPTER 6

Naboth's Vineyard

Psalms 23:4-6 (NLT)

⁴ Even when I walk through the darkest valley, I will not be afraid, for you are close beside me. Your rod and your staff protect and comfort me. ⁵ You prepare a feast for me in the presence of my enemies. You honor me by anointing my head with oil. My cup overflows with blessings. ⁶ Surely your goodness and unfailing love will pursue me all the days of my life, and I will live in the house of the LORD forever.

Have you ever had to stand up for yourself, even if it may cost you your life? Sometimes you have to do the very thing you don't want to do. Even if you have to do it afraid. I remember telling myself that enough was enough. I didn't want to go through the abuse anymore, the fear, the sexual abuse, the feeling of feeling unloved, and the silent treatment. I remember sneaking into the pantry at night, afraid to get a snack. If I were caught, I would have to hear my ex's mouth about how late it was for me to get a snack. He often reminded me that I would fix my dinner plate portions the size of a man's plate. I would try hard not to overeat or put less on my plate. Even after I divorced and remarried, I would catch myself sneaking into the pantry to get a snack and slowly opening the package so my husband wouldn't hear the wrapper opening. Looking back on that now, I know that I was reliving the fear I once had. It took me back to when I thought I had escaped. This was the trauma that I was experiencing. I experienced many episodes and had to receive inner healing through my pastor.

When you leave trauma open, and you don't get healing in the situation, you will find yourself reliving the situation. Please **GO GET INNER HEALING**.

I did attempt to leave this abusive marriage multiple times. My heart would be racing out of fear. I didn't want to be caught. I remember one incident when I was slung into the door because I had his phone going through it. It was a late Friday or Saturday night, and he was getting ready to go out. I knew that he was about to go out and cheat. I saw an opportunity, he had left his phone in the den on the couch. I went for it and went to the bathroom and locked the door. I started to go through the text, and there I saw him texting another woman. I was hurt, and I started to text back, pretending to be him. I then heard knocks at the door and heard him saying he needed to come in and get some deodorant. I told him to get it from the other bathroom. He then began to pick the locks on the door. He eventually makes his way in, reaches for his phone, and I pull back. The next thing I knew, I was slung into the door, and I yelled that I was going to call the cops. He let me go and said that I don't have any marks on me. I called the cops and told them what was happening, and they came out. By this time, he was gone.

The next day, he came back and the silent treatment began. I knew I couldn't stay there because of the fear that I felt and the hatred that I had. I wanted to be with my family, and away from the home I was in. I remember my ex going to work, and I planned my escape. I went and took my kids out of school, withdrew money from the bank, got on the road to Ohio in my blue Saturn, and drove through the night. I called my mom on the way and told her what had happened. It was by the grace of God that I made it there.

After I arrived in Ohio, I filed a protection order, transferred my job, and got a place. I did it all in one day. My family helped me furnish the place, and I lived comfortably with my kids. This victory was short-lived. About four months later, we had a court date in Ohio that didn't go my way, and then we had a court date in Tallahassee. I was forced to send my kids back to Tallahassee. Which meant I had to go back to Tallahassee. There was no way I was sending my kids back, so I stayed. This was the most painful experience I had to go through. I was sent back without my family and left to do this alone.

I didn't know God at that time. I knew of Him but had no relationship with Him. Looking back through this whole process, I see that God was still covering me through the process.

You may be asking yourself how this relates to Naboth's Vineyard. Well, what I did was stand up for myself against my abuser. I had so much fear going on inside me. I was terrified of the outcome, but I pressed through. Even though I felt extremely weak, I was made strong through Christ. Many nights, I didn't understand why the courts made me return. As I sit here now, I feel in my Spirit that God allowed me to stay home for those four months to be nursed by my family before He sent me back for the journey I had to go through. Just like Elijah. He left for a season and then faced the problem again. Just because God allows you to be sent back to a place of hurt, it's not to destroy you, and it doesn't mean that God don't love you, but it's to grow you for what's to come. If I weren't sent back to Tallahassee, I wouldn't be the woman of God that I am today. Now let's look at the story of Naboth:

1 KINGS 21 1-15 NLT

¹ *Now there was a man named Naboth, from Jezreel, who owned a vineyard in Jezreel beside the palace of King Ahab of Samaria.* ² *One day Ahab said to Naboth, "Since your vineyard is so convenient to my palace, I would like to buy it to use as a vegetable garden. I will give you a better vineyard in exchange, or if you prefer, I will pay you for it."* ³ *But Naboth replied, "The Lord forbid that I should give you the inheritance that was passed down by my ancestors."* ⁴ *So Ahab went home angry and sullen because of Naboth's answer. The king went to bed with his face to the wall and refused to eat!* ⁵ *"What's the matter?" his wife Jezebel asked him. "What's made you so upset that you're not eating?"* ⁶ *"I asked Naboth to sell me his vineyard or trade it, but he refused!" Ahab told her.* ⁷ *"Are you the king of Israel or not?" Jezebel demanded. "Get up and eat something, and don't worry about it. I'll get you Naboth's vineyard!"* ⁸ *So she wrote letters in Ahab's name, sealed them with his seal, and sent them to the elders and other leaders of the town where Naboth lived.* ⁹ *In her letters she commanded: "Call the citizens together for a time of fasting, and give Naboth a place of honor.* ¹⁰ *And then seat two scoundrels across from him who will accuse him of cursing God and the king. Then take him out and stone him to death."* ¹¹ *So the elders and other town leaders followed the instructions Jezebel had written in the letters.* ¹² *They called for a fast and put Naboth at a prominent place before the people.*

13 Then the two scoundrels came and sat down across from him. And they accused Naboth before all the people, saying, "He cursed God and the king." So he was dragged outside the town and stoned to death. 14 The town leaders then sent word to Jezebel, "Naboth has been stoned to death." 15 When Jezebel heard the news, she said to Ahab, "You know the vineyard Naboth wouldn't sell you? Well, you can have it now! He's dead!" 16 So Ahab immediately went down to the vineyard of Naboth to claim it.

We see that Ahab was plotting and scheming to get Naboth's Vineyard. He even tries to offer Naboth something for the vineyard. Naboth stood his ground and said no because the Lord forbade him to give his family's inheritance.

When you tell a person dealing with this spirit of Ahab **"NO,"** you need to know that Jezebel is not too far from him. The Ahab spirit isn't as strong as Jezebel's. We also have to recognize that the spirit of Jezebel is operating with the spirit of Baal, which was mentioned at the beginning of the book. Anytime you tell a person that is carrying this spirit "no" you have to expect some severe backlash. They will go to great lengths to get what they want from you. In most cases, they will find out what you love the most and attack that very thing. If it's your workplace, they will destroy it, and if it's your kids, they will attack that too.

In my case, my kids were the choice of weapon Just to name a couple of incidents. I was being attacked through any government assistance I was getting. He would try to apply for food stamps knowing I was already receiving them. Anyone that receives food stamps knows that two people with the same kids can't both apply for and get food stamps. He would call to get them to take the food stamps from me by making false allegations. Even though he knew I had no help and no family near me. He would not cooperate or follow the parenting plan given to us by the courts. So I would take him to court.

I have been to court more than I can count. I later realized that my taking him to court was a game. As my relationship with God got serious, God showed me that he was purposely not following the plan because he knew I would take him to court. I eventually stopped because I realized that no matter how many times the judge waved her finger and found him in contempt, he would do the same thing repeatedly. Right, when I stopped taking him to court, he then started to take me to court. Later he used my kids and caused them to run away. It happened overnight it seemed. One minute, my son and I were bonding, and the next time he came home, it was like a curse was placed on him. My son was not my son. I saw pure evilness, and I knew that it was a spirit of rage that had taken over him. Watching my son react in that manner hurt me so badly. I cried many days and many nights. I hated my life and the entire situation. I remember pulling away from God instead of getting closer to Him. Years later, I had to relive the same situation but less intensely. My second son was corrupted, and he decided to follow after his brother. I don't blame my boys, but I blame the demonic forces behind it.

Jezebel planned and plotted and eventually got what she wanted. Naboth died, and Jezebel got what her husband wanted: "The Vineyard". Like my situation, my ex got what he wanted, " My Kids." But we must remember that in the end, Jezebel always plays her hand too much, and the victory that she thought she had is/was short-lived. I know this will be my fate as well.

Please understand that you are not supposed to bow down to this spirit. God said in His word that if you tolerate this woman, Jezebel, then I will throw you on a sick bed with her (**Read Revelation 2:20-22**). I don't care what it looks like or feels like; **DON'T GIVE IN**. When you have done all you can do, then stand still. Vengeance belongs to the Lord. It's only a matter of time before the spirit messes up. Note: Even when they mess up and are wrong/caught in the wrong they do, they don't take responsibility.

THINGS TO REMEMBER:

1. Don't allow the Jezebel Spirit to control you.
2. Remember that the spirit will go after the very thing you love and cherish the most.
3. Don't lose hope and your faith.
4. Even if it costs you something, everything will be ok.
5. Where there is an Ahab, there is a Jezebel.
6. This spirit overplays its hand.
7. Jezebel always has people working for her (the spirit isn't generalized and can work through a man or female, young or old).
8. This spirit is manipulative in getting what they want.
9. This spirit doesn't follow rules.
10. Get closer to God during this difficult time.

CHAPTER 7

Seductive Jezebel

MATTHEW 5:28 (NLT)

But I say, anyone who even looks at a woman with lust has already committed adultery with her in his heart.

M any scriptures in the Bible tell us not to lust and that if we look upon a woman with our eyes, we have already committed adultery (**Read Matthew 5:28**).

This also goes for women. You may ask yourself, what do you do when you find yourself looking? I was on TikTok, and this video came up. There was a man who was in the gym, and he was talking about how he defeated the enemy with perversive thoughts. He said that he invited God into his thoughts. He tells God the issues, and he prays to God about the thought that is taking place in his mind.

2 CORINTHIANS 10:5 - 6

⁵ Casting down arguments and every high thing that exalts itself against the knowledge of God, bringing every thought into captivity to the obedience of Christ, ⁶ and being ready to punish all disobedience when your obedience is fulfilled.

What this scripture is telling us to cast the thought down. But instead, some people meditate on the thought, and then the thought makes its way to your heart. Next thing, the person is acting out the thought through their actions. This can be a physical, mental, or verbal reaction. Have you ever seen a person who was fully demonically possessed? I have, and they are not in control of their behavior. That's because they didn't seek help, cast their thoughts out, or turn their life over to God. I'm sure there are many other reasons but those come to mind.

Let me share one of my experiences with you. I was in the gym one day, and I was about to walk out to leave. I have been there for some time but felt the urge to get on the treadmill. As I was on the treadmill, I heard the lady next to me (about two treadmills in between), and she was yelling at the top of her lungs. She was cussing and verbally talking about her son being molested. She sounded like she could have been on the phone with a relative. I immediately began to cast that demon down, binding and losing it. The noise continued, and later, a gym worker got on the treadmill beside her and told her that she had to keep it down or she would be asked to leave. He was nice to her about it. I felt the urge to go next to her after the guy left, and I walked over, got on the treadmill, and started talking to her about the things I heard her talking about. She was much calmer and responded to what I was saying. I even offered prayer. The point I'm making is you have the same authority and power to stop the enemy from attacking your mind. If you bind and lose those demons, you would be able to stop the attack. Those spirits who have had legal rights to use her had to recognize the power I came in.

They have to subject themselves to the spirit of God. This is the same way that you stop your mind from thinking freely about the enemy's thoughts. Here are some ways to help you get through the temptations and thinking that may come your way.

1. Pray and invite the Holy Spirit to take complete control of your thoughts.

2. Quote/remember 2 Corinthians 10:5 every time an ungodly thought or emotion comes.

3. Replace the thoughts and emotions with the word of God. This may require you to write down scriptures that pertain to your situation.

4. Ask yourself what the root problem is and why this thought continues to happen.

5. Find out what the open door is that gives satan and his demons legal rights.

6. Pray and ask God for forgiveness and to close all sinful doors you have opened up.

7. You may need inner healing and deliverance.

8. Fasting.

9. Attending church regularly.

WAYS YOU KNOW THAT YOU MAY NEED INNER HEALING AND DELIVERANCE:

1. No matter what you do, you can't control your emotion or behavior.

2. If you had past trauma and accidents that happened to you.

3. If you have stress and depression that overtakes you and you can't come out of it.

4. If you blank out and can't remember what happened/ feel like something overtakes your body even when you are fighting against it.

5. You experience physical manifestations that you cannot control. Such as shaking, body or eye rolling, screaming, the feeling that something is in your throat, headaches, horrible thoughts and vomiting just to name a few.

6. An uncontrolled anger that causes you to lose control and break things and hurt people.

7. Lie uncontrollably.

8. You have incubus and succubus (sexual dreams) while sleeping and reach an orgasm "wet dream."

9. If you have been diagnosed with multiple personalities schizophrenia or been in a mental institution.

10. You practice sin and can't seem to stop.

11. You don't see the fruits of the spirit in your life even though you follow God.

12. You see a pattern of issues in your family (generational curse), whether disease, poverty, anger, divorce, miscarriage, sexual perversion, drugs, alcohol, teen pregnancy, rape, and other issues.

13. Constantly sick, and in most cases, the doctor can't find anything wrong.

Please note that these are just a few, and there are many other signs

OBVIOUS SIGNS THAT JEZEBEL IS IN YOUR BLOODLINE:

1. If people "mainly women" have been raped or molested.

   - For most of all deliverances that my husband and I have done, Jezebel has been present. Most of the time, the spirit comes in through rape and molestation.

2. If people in your family are constantly manipulating and lying.

3. Family discord.

HERE ARE A FEW SIGNS THAT YOU MAY HAVE THE SPIRIT OF JEZEBEL IN YOU.

Please note that if you only have a couple of these then that doesn't mean you have the Spirit, you could just be dealing with issues that need to be addressed. However, if you notice that you are checking off everything and leaving a few then it's a high chance that you are operating with the spirit of Jezebel and you need deliverance. I am a deliverance pastor and would love to help you get free. Please go to *bethelight.live* if you need inner healing and or deliverance.

1. When your growth has come to a halt.

2. When you have no motivation to grow or keep a relationship with God.

3. You don't submit to authority.

4. You attack those that don't do what you want.

5. You are manipulative and controlling.

6. It must be your way or the highway.

7. You feel like you can't control your actions even though you know it's wrong.

8. You have no emotions.

9. You don't care how others feel.

10. You can't sympathize with people's emotions and feelings.

11. It's all about you.

12. You will make people pay for their actions toward you and will go to great lengths.

13. You were raped and haven't dealt with the issue.

14. If you are a woman: You don't submit to male authority.

15. You must be in charge.

16. You are lustful and seductive.

17. You have an addiction.

When you break these curses, receive inner healing, and go through deliverance, you set yourself free and your kids, grandkids, etc., free. It is time to set the entire bloodline free. Are you a generational curse breaker?

I remember when I was out in the world, I would use my body and looks to get what I wanted. I would dress nice 'very little clothed", put on my perfume and heels, and have my hair cute. I would use my looks to seduce men and get them to buy me a drink. Once I got what I wanted, I would move on to the next. Friday and Saturday nights allowed me to go out, sin and have a good time. Let's admit it. When you were in the world, it was fun and exciting. The thought of living on the edge was high. I would meet guys and let them take me out to get a free meal and maybe a movie depending on how they looked. I escorted myself. After I dated them for a bit, I ended up sleeping with a few (not all), then cut the relationship short. I was told that I acted like a man. I had no emotions tied to the men I was sleeping with, but they were drawing a connection to me for some reason. I wasn't the typical woman they were used to. Little did I know I was carrying a demon called Jezebel. Jezebel has changed my character and the person God has called me to be. To know more about what I have been through, please get my other book, My Journey To Salvation.

HOW DID THE SPIRIT GET IN ME, MANY MAY ASK?

1. I was raped.
2. I was molested.
3. I was in a relationship that sexually abused me.
4. Porn.
5. Masturbation.
6. Soul Ties.
7. I was sexual with people that had this spirit.
8. I opened myself up to it.

This spirit had legal access to me since I was born. My other family members (females) have also been raped and molested. It's a generational curse on the bloodline. Did you know when a person dies and has not broken the curse or received deliverance, the demons left in the person go to the next available family, this is one reason the spirit can be in the family for many generations. This makes the spirit stronger over the years and passes in the generation. This is something I learned through Bob Larson. He has a book called Jezebel, which goes into great detail about the spirit. I highly recommend the book.

CHAPTER 8

Jezebel Death

REVELATION 2:20-23 (NLT)

20 "But I have this complaint against you. You are permitting that woman--that Jezebel who calls herself a prophet--to lead my servants astray. She teaches them to commit sexual sin and to eat food offered to idols. 21 I gave her time to repent, but she does not want to turn away from her immorality.
22 "Therefore, I will throw her on a bed of suffering, and those who commit adultery with her will suffer greatly unless they repent and turn away from her evil deeds. 23 I will strike her children dead. Then all the churches will know that I am the one who searches out the thoughts and intentions of every person. And I will give to each of you whatever you deserve.

Anytime you are dealing with a spirit in a person, you have to come to grips with the fact that you can't have fear. Elijah ran from Jezebel and hid in a cave after he had a significant victory.

How many times have you hidden from something after you had won? Maybe for you, it was a court case, but you ran in fear of the other person's reaction. Maybe it was a competition of some sort. Regardless of what it was, when you come up against the spirit of Jezebel, this spirit will try to get victory over you even if you have already won. This spirit is also a spirit of intimidation and will use others to do their work just like Jezebel did. Maybe your kids were used against you, your spouse, your job, or a family member. People will turn their back on you. You never thought they would do so. I had to face many attacks and my kids had been used as a weapon against me. After countless court cases and wins, I still felt like I had lost the battle. It wasn't until I got close to God and developed a relationship with Him that I realized I was fighting this battle wrongly. Anytime you try to fight a spiritual battle in the flesh, you will always lose. Every battle starts in the spiritual realm, which means you have to fight in the spiritual realm.

NOW LET'S EXAMINE JEZEBEL'S FINAL MOMENT IN

2 KING 9:30-37

30 *Now when Jehu had come to Jezreel, Jezebel heard of it; and she put paint on her eyes and adorned her head, and looked through a window.* 31 *Then, as Jehu entered at the gate, she said, "Is it peace, Zimri, murderer of your master?"* 32 *And he looked up at the window, and said, "Who is on my side? Who?" So two or three eunuchs looked out at him.* 33 *Then he said, "Throw her down." So they threw her down, and some of her blood spattered on the wall and on the horses; and he trampled her underfoot.* 34 *And when he had gone in, he ate and drank. Then he said, "Go now, see to this accursed woman, and bury her, for she was a king's daughter."* 35 *So they went to bury her, but they found no more of her than the skull and the feet and the palms of her hands.* 36 *Therefore they came back and told him. And he said, "This is the word of the Lord, which He spoke by His servant Elijah the Tishbite, saying, 'On the plot of ground at Jezreel dogs shall eat the flesh of Jezebel;* 37 *and the corpse of Jezebel shall be as refuse on the surface of the field, in the plot at Jezreel, so that they shall not say, "Here lies Jezebel."*

Notice the first thing she did was prepare herself to look nice. I asked myself if she did this to seduce Jehu or to look nice before she died. I have heard many pastors preach both. Jezebel also asks, **"Is it peace, Zimri, murderer of your master?"** that never gets answered. Jehu ignored her, asked how many were on his side, and then told them to throw her out of the window. It was judgment day for Jezebel. She harmed, placed fear, and caused God's people to flee. Jehu came with authority, and he came to finish the work of God. Two or three eunuchs threw her down, and she spattered on the wall and the horses. She got destroyed that day and wasn't recognizable. God will destroy the Jezebel in your life but you must take it to the spiritual realm and don't react to what they do to you in the natural realm.

Are you ready to finish the work of God?

Are you ready to destroy Satan and his evil plans?

Are you ready to destroy Jezebel?

TAKEAWAYS FROM THIS SCRIPTURE

1. Don't back down from Jezebel.
2. Don't respond to the non-sense that Jezebel offers.
3. Keep your focus on God.
4. Finish the work God called you to, no matter how afraid you are. **DO IT AFRAID**, if you have to.

I remember making the hardest decision in my life. I had to choose to go through a divorce that I knew would hurt many in the process. I battled with if I stay what the results would be long term and if I go, what the effects would be long-term. I knew that whatever I decided, I would have to stick with my choice and not waver. Listening to many people and being in fear caused me to be mentally drained. I was 120 lbs, I was physically sick. I have never been so small. It was hard to eat food. I was stressed and depressed, and I drank a lot. I was also mentally drained. I tried to leave multiple times before but ended up coming back. I came back because of fear and because I didn't realize that the person was operating under demonic influence. Every time I would leave, I would be set on "I'm not going back," and somehow, the smooth talk and the emotions that came with it drew me back shortly after, I would find myself regretting going back and upset with the world that I went back to. The hurt I caused my kids from the back and forth was the deepest pain that I felt. They are still paying the price for the many mistakes I made.

When you face a hard choice in life, you will have to pull your strength from God. Don't add more sorrow to your pain. You have to draw from the source that created you. That source is Jesus. The living water, the Alpha and Omega, the beginning and the end.

Learning to lean on God was one of the hardest lessons I had to learn. I felt like the Israelites. They went on an 11-day journey, and it took them 40 years. They just couldn't get it right. They complained, and they made idols for themselves. Generation after generation, they circled the trail over and over again. What number of years is this for you? How often does God have to speak to you about getting it right the next time? I finally started to understand years later after my divorce took place.

Let me explain: After I got a divorce, I didn't turn my life around, I didn't get saved, I didn't go to church, I wasn't fasting and praying, and I wasn't seeking help from all the trauma, and damage I went through. However, I turned my life over to the devil more than ever before and lived a sinful/unrighteous lifestyle. I drank, partied, had sex, cussed, watched awful movies, listened to horrible music, and took sleeping pills. Instead of trying to get close to God, I was farther away from Him than ever before. This journey took me about two years until I hit rock bottom. You would think after the divorce, I was already at rock bottom, but I wasn't.

As I had my last sexual interaction with this guy, I remember thinking I didn't want to do this. This man lured me into having sex with him. He was someone I knew, and when he came to town, we would hang out. We never did anything because, honestly, I didn't want to or have any desire to. He would mention it, but I would always turn it down and go my separate way. One day he came to town and asked to shower at my place "We just got done working out." I felt that I should say no, but I said ok. Well, the next thing I know, he's asking for a massage and pursuing sex. I wanted to say no so badly, but for some reason, I couldn't. It's like I was paralyzed and just went with it. I remember I couldn't wait for it to be over. When it was over, he left. I caused myself more harm, damage, and soul ties and received more demons. Looking back on the situation, I was controlled by the spirit of Jezebel and so many others. The last guy I was with before I met my husband had a lust demon, which is why I felt paralyzed. Also, the past life experience I had (rape and molestation) caused me to be paralyzed. That spirit was trying to stay around me and still do up to this day. It's called a "familiar spirit," and it tries to monitor me so that it can report to the demonic realm what I'm doing. The information can also be given to witches and warlocks. The person the demon is using typically has no idea they are being used.

After that last experience, I remember thinking he was the last one I would sleep with and that I couldn't do this anymore. I began to feel the conviction, and it weighed on me heavily. It wasn't until shortly after that I went back to church and my life slowly changed.

This was almost a two-year process that I went through. Years later, I had to learn how to forgive, how to trust God and have faith, how to love the way God loves, how to fast, to pray, and to turn from my sinful lifestyle. I had to receive God as my Lord and Savior, had to repent, had to get rid of toxic people in my life, had to learn to run to God and not the courts, had to go to church and learn how to have a relationship with God, I had to learn how to cope with my problems without alcohol and sleeping pills. I also went through inner healing and deliverance, and so much more. This process took 8 to 9 years. I am so grateful for where I am now. Looking back, I'm sure my time could have been cut in half, but I chose to do things my way first before trying God.

When you don't face this spirit head-on, you will suffer mentally, emotionally, sexually (for some), and physically. This spirit don't give up until it's defeated through death, just like Jezebel. If a person is carrying this spirit and they don't repent and get deliverance, this spirit will destroy them and everything they put their hands on, especially relationships. That spirit will break up marriages and the relationship that they have with their kids and family. God's word says **Revelation 2:20-23 NLT**

> [20] *"But I have this complaint against you. You are permitting that woman—that Jezebel who calls herself a prophet—to lead my servants astray. She teaches them to commit sexual sin and to eat food offered to idols.* [21] *I gave her time to repent, but she does not want to turn away from her immorality.* [22]

> "Therefore, I will throw her on a bed of suffering,[c] and those who commit adultery with her will suffer greatly unless they repent and turn away from her evil deeds. 23 I will strike her children dead. Then all the churches will know that I am the one who searches out the thoughts and intentions of every person. And I will give to each of you whatever you deserve.

God tells us to repent and turn away from her evil deeds. When you stay around or with a person that has this spirit, you will reap the punishment that the person with this spirit will receive. Let's examine the scripture:

1. First, God had a complaint against you (for tolerating the spirit) for all the evil deeds it's causing/caused.

2. God gave her time to repent (but she refused).

3. God gave punishment for her and those who commit adultery with her (agreeing with her).

4. If you agree with a person that has this spirit by not leaving the situation, you are committing adultery with her.

5. The punishment for those who don't turn away from this spirit is to suffer greatly.

6. The kids of the person with this spirit will also suffer greatly.

This is one spirit that comes with harsh punishment. If you don't stand up to this spirit, it will destroy you. I remember each encounter I had with this spirit produced great fear.. Fear would present itself before I had to interact with the person. I would ask myself why this fear is so strong and why can't I control it. The more you stand up to the person with this spirit, the more you will see victory. Remember, you have to fight this in the spiritual realm.

The Start Of My Victory

One night, I decided to pray and petition God about this spirit and what it was doing to my family and me. I asked God to arrest this spirit so that it couldn't bother me again. I used God's word "scripture" to petition God about what was taking place. I went to bed, and that night, this big demon was floating over my bed and asked, "How could you? " and I woke up. I knew then that God had answered my prayer. I woke up and felt the victory.

To Defeat This Spirit, You Must:

1. Stand for what is right.
2. You must confront the demon in the spiritual realm.
3. Stand firm in your word.
4. Pray often.
5. Fast often because you will need your strength.
6. Remember that you have the victory.
7. Petition God for your safety from this spirit.
8. Don't lose hope.
9. Don't give in to the person that has this spirit.
10. Use your spiritual weapons.

SPIRITUAL WEAPONS TO USE (NLT)

1. Pleading the blood of Jesus and testifying

REVELATION 12:11 (NLT)

And they have defeated him by the blood of the Lamb and by their testimony. And they did not love their lives so much that they were afraid to die.

2. Using Scripture

JEREMIAH 23:29 (NLT)

Does not my word burn like fire?" says the LORD. "Is it not like a mighty hammer that smashes a rock to pieces?

3. Losing and binding

MATTHEW 18:18-20 (NLT)

[18] "I tell you the truth, whatever you forbid on earth will be forbidden in heaven, and whatever you permit on earth will be permitted in heaven. [19] "I also tell you this: If two of you agree here on earth concerning anything you ask, my Father in heaven will do it for you. [20] For where two or three gather together as my followers, I am there among them."

4. Calling thunder apon the enemy

1 SAMUEL 7:10 (NLT)

Just as Samuel was sacrificing the burnt offering, the Philistines arrived to attack Israel. But the LORD spoke with a mighty voice of thunder from heaven that day, and the Philistines were thrown into such confusion that the Israelites defeated them.

5. The name of Jesus

PHILIPPIANS 2:9-11 (NLT)

9 Therefore, God elevated him to the place of highest honor and gave him the name above all other names, 10 that at the name of Jesus every knee should bow, in heaven and on earth and under the earth, 11 and every tongue confess that Jesus Christ is Lord, to the glory of God the Father.

6. Speaking in tongues

ROMANS 8:26-27 (NLT)

26 And the Holy Spirit helps us in our weakness. For example, we don't know what God wants us to pray for. But the Holy Spirit prays for us with groaning that cannot be expressed in words. 27 And the Father who knows all hearts knows what the Spirit is saying, for the Spirit pleads for us believers in harmony with God's own will.

7. Pulling down strongholds

2 CORINTHIANS 10:3-5 (NLT)

> [3] *We are human, but we don't wage war as humans do.* [4] *We use God's mighty weapons, not worldly weapons, to knock down the strongholds of human reasoning and to destroy false arguments.* [5] *We destroy every proud obstacle that keeps people from knowing God. We capture their rebellious thoughts and teach them to obey Christ*

8. Praying without ceasing

1 THESSALONIANS 5:16-18 (NLT)

> [16] *Always be joyful.* [17] *Never stop praying.* [18] *Be thankful in all circumstances, for this is God's will for you who belong to Christ Jesus.*

9. Angles of war

2 KINGS 19:35 (NLT)

> *That night the angel of the LORD went out to the Assyrian camp and killed 185,000 Assyrian soldiers. When the surviving Assyrians woke up the next morning, they found corpses everywhere.*

10. Asking God to confuse/panic the enemy

EXODUS 23:27 (NLT)

"I will send my terror ahead of you and create panic among all the people whose lands you invade. I will make all your enemies turn and run.

11. Decree and declare

PSALMS 2:6-7 (NLT)

6 For the Lord declares, "I have placed my chosen king on the throne in Jerusalem, on my holy mountain." 7 The king proclaims the LORD's decree: "The LORD said to me, 'You are my son. Today I have become your Father.

12. Holy Ghost fire

2 KINGS 1:10 (NLT)

But Elijah replied to the captain, "If I am a man of God, let fire come down from heaven and destroy you and your fifty men!" Then fire fell from heaven and killed them all.

13. Fasting

ISAIAH 58:6 (NLT)

"No, this is the kind of fasting I want: Free those who are wrongly imprisoned; lighten the burden of those who work for you. Let the oppressed go free, and remove the chains that bind people.

EZRA 8:23 (NLT)

So we fasted and earnestly prayed that our God would take care of us, and he heard our prayer.

14. Release the hounds

1 KINGS 21:23 (NLT)

"And regarding Jezebel, the LORD says, 'Dogs will eat Jezebel's body at the plot of land in Jezreel.'

15. Cause an earthquake in the enemy camp

1 SAMUEL 14:15 (NLT)

Suddenly, panic broke out in the Philistine army, both in the camp and in the field, including even the outposts and raiding parties. And just then an earthquake struck, and everyone was terrified.

16. Hailstones on the enemy

JOSHUA 10:11 (NLT)

As the Amorites retreated down the road from Beth-horon, the LORD destroyed them with a terrible hailstorm from heaven that continued until they reached Azekah. The hail killed more of the enemy than the Israelites killed with the sword.

17. Whirlwind

JEREMIAH 23:19 (NLT)

Look! The LORD's anger bursts out like a storm, a whirlwind that swirls down on the heads of the wicked.

18. Cause the enemy to have no rest

JOSHUA 10:19 (NLT)

The rest of you continue chasing the enemy and cut them down from the rear. Don't give them a chance to get back to their towns, for the LORD your God has given you victory over them."

19. Sword of God

EZEKIEL 21:3-5 (NLT)

³ Tell her, 'This is what the LORD says: I am your enemy, O Israel, and I am about to unsheath my sword to destroy your people--the righteous and the wicked alike. ⁴ Yes, I will cut off both the righteous and the wicked! I will draw my sword against everyone in the land from south to north. ⁵ Everyone in the world will know that I am the LORD. My sword is in my hand, and it will not return to its sheath until its work is finished.'

20. Ask God to release the locust

EXODUS 10:3-6 (NLT)

³ So Moses and Aaron went to Pharaoh and said, "This is what the LORD, the God of the Hebrews, says: How long will you refuse to submit to me? Let my people go, so they can worship me. ⁴ If you refuse, watch out! For tomorrow I will bring a swarm of locusts on your country. ⁵ They will cover the land so that you won't be able to see the ground. They will devour what little is left of your crops after the hailstorm, including all the trees growing in the fields. ⁶ They will overrun your palaces and the homes of your officials and all the houses in Egypt. Never in the history of Egypt have your ancestors seen a plague like this one!" And with that, Moses turned and left Pharaoh.

21. Ask God to send lightning

PSALMS 77:18 (NLT)

Your thunder roared from the whirlwind; the lightning lit up the world! The earth trembled and shook.

CHAPTER 9

Freedom From Jezebel,
Fear & Anxiety

JOHN 8:36 (NKJV)

"Therefore if the Son makes you free, you shall be free indeed.

I would like to think that the fear and anxiety left right immediately, but it didn't. Years passed by, and in 2022 I remember the day it left me. The stronghold that it had over me left me. I felt a huge release. Let me take you through this journey and an amazing day.

It was sometime in Dec. 2021 I was at the gym working out. I remember getting this feeling over me that I needed to call home and check on the boys, but I didn't. I was almost done working out, so I finished and headed home. As I walked through my front door, I felt something wasn't right. I was talking to my youngest son, and then I asked him where his brother was. He told me that he doesn't know and may be in the back. As I walked back there, the Holy Spirit told me he had run away. As much as I didn't want to believe it, I knew what God had told me was true. I continued to the back and I searched around for him and then I ran back to the front and asked his brother again. Then he told me what had happened. I knew I was about to face another roller coaster/ hurdle I had to face years prior. Because my oldest son ran away. That situation just about made me feel close to death and now this one felt like I was being stabbed in my chest. The hurt, betrayal, confusion, and pain I felt came all at once that it would have taken an unbeliever out. All I could think was how he could do this to me and why he didn't just talk to me about his feelings. I had just talked to my son weeks prior and told him that he would never have to run, and to talk to me if he wanted to stay at his dad's. He assured me that he didn't want that.

Moments after finding out he ran away, I checked to see if his dad wrote in the parenting app to tell me if he had him and he did. He mentioned that he would be at the gas station waiting on me to return my son to me. He gave me a time that he would leave if I didn't show up. Which by the way he never waited. He just left according to the gas station footage and people that worked there. As I reached the gas station, I asked the people questions about my son and if they had seen him. They told me that he waited around a bit and he told them somebody was on the way to get him.

Meanwhile, I had my two other kids with me looking for their brother. One had tears in their eyes and the other seemed to be over it. I continued on this goose chase for about an hour and did everything to get him back but God told me he was not coming back, their dad is lying, and to check the camera footage. It hit me and I thought to myself that's right I have cameras. I went home mad, angry, hurt, and thinking I can't believe I'm going through this again. As I drove home without my son, I knew he wouldn't be back soon and that his father was trying to take my kids from me simply because I stood up for myself and refused to be abused by that spirit. When I got home I check the footage and sure enough, it wasn't to my surprise that his dad plotted, manipulated, controlled, and skimmed the idea of "running away." Not only did I hear it on the camera but I felt it in my spirit. Just as he had done in the past.

What you have to understand about this spirit is when you say no or do the opposite of what the spirit wants you to do, the spirit will find a way for you to pay. It will go after everything you love and use it as a weapon. Since I was no longer in the household and Jezebel couldn't control me as it used to, it used my kids. My kids became the bullets that fired at me.

THE COURT HEARING

I ended up having an emergency hearing to get my son back. I even presented every piece of evidence and it seemed like the judge could care less. She ordered that my son get back on the parenting rotation and that he wasn't old enough to make that choice. However, my son was convinced he didn't have to return.

The day after the court hearing, I went to pick my son up from school. God had already told me he wouldn't be coming home with me. God was right. I went to pick him up in the car pick up, and he refused to get in. He said he didn't have to, and the cops couldn't make him. These were the same words and actions that his brother had done years before. I knew that my son had been brainwashed with lies.

So, I got out of my truck, and I talked with my son, and God brought up the scripture *1 Corinthians 13;4-8*

> ⁴ *Love is patient and kind; love does not envy or boast; it is not arrogant 5 or rude. It does not insist on its own way; it is not irritable or resentful;[b]* ⁶ *it does not rejoice at wrongdoing, but rejoices with the truth.* ⁷ *Love bears all things, believes all things, hopes all things, endures all things.* ⁸ *Love never ends. As for prophecies, they will pass away; as for tongues, they will cease; as for knowledge, it will pass away.*

At that moment, God was telling me to let him go. God told me it didn't matter what the court said, how I felt, or what his father had done to manipulate the situation. God was showing me that I have to let him see for himself. With tears in my eyes, I read my son that scripture and hugged him, and told him that love is patient and longsuffering. I also told him that I love him and that he was always welcomed home. When I asked him why he ran away he said he just wanted to stay with dad because it's more fun, he can learn how to be a man, and he can do more over there. The cop that was standing by was also shocked at his answers and told him that there are kids that wish they can see their moms and wished someone loved them like I did. I felt like I lost my son that day over "fun & manipulation"But when I walked away, the spirit of fear lifted from me and I felt God heal me in the midst of me feeling broken. I was then facing what seemed to be a loss and victory all in one.

I received my freedom back that day. Jezebel expected me to act differently but I chose to live, and I chose to love my other kids and be a mom to the ones who wanted me to be a mom. That day I went home, me and my other kids went out to eat, and I loved on them. Yes, I felt hurt, but I chose to be free. God also showed me that he gave me more time with my kids than the time I was losing and have lost. God began to show me that there were areas in my life that I still needed to heal from and that this was a part of that journey.

THE APOLOGY

It was one late night around 2 a.m. and I was up praying. God laid it on my heart that I needed to apologize to my kid's father, his sister, and his parents. Now I must admit I was crying like a baby. I was asking God why and telling Him I didn't do anything. I had so many excuses. I couldn't even put the words together to even write. As I sat there with praise and worship music playing, God began to give me the words to say. One by one I wrote the letters and one by one I hit send. This was extremely hard to do because I didn't understand why God wanted me to say sorry. Especially after all the attacks I received from that family. I can't say that I processed this overnight but I do remember God started to speak to me on how I was handling things. God told me that I had to lighten up and allow the kids to spend time with their grandparents if I didn't have anything planned and that if it benefits the kids then let them do it. It wasn't easy at first but I knew it was necessary. God had shown me that I was being controlled by trying not to be controlled and manipulated by the kid's father and the family. God told me that even if things are done to manipulate, I shouldn't worry about it just look to see if it benefits the kids.

Unfortunately, I had to have two of my kids taken from me for me to get the big picture. I had to go through this season year after year to see that I was in error myself. Looking back on this so much could have been avoided. I'm just thankful that I understand now what God was trying to show me.

After hitting send (text message for the apologies) weeks and maybe even a month later, I spoke to the aunt first and then the grandparents and we started to communicate from there. Their dad wasn't on board, he never responded to the message which I didn't expect him to, I never wrote the apologies for a response, but I now know I wrote the apology to release what's been keeping me hostage. Shortly after I was able to be at my son's 13 birthday party that they gave him and we all talked and the kids had a chance to see us getting along. It was a beautiful thing. I also didn't have any fear or anxiety present.

Freedom

I am now free from this tormenting spirit. I am no longer controlled by something that once had its grip around my neck slowly trying to kill me. It almost drained me **BUT God showed up for me**. 2022 is the year that I got back my freedom and it's also the year that I chose to press through each day. I chose to think of the positive, regardless of what it looks like. I chose to not be afraid of what others may think. I chose to live again and do what I can for my boys while they are with me. I thank God for giving me more time with them than I have lost. I thank God for giving me the years that are the most important. God showed me that even Jesus left his parent's home at the age of 12. Yes, it was under a different circumstance but God showed me that all the nurturing that was needed was done. God showed me that they have a foundation to come back to. I had to learn to trust God even more and know that God loves my boys more than I do. God had to remind me of all the promises He has shown me and that they will come to pass.

Finally, I knew that the cycle has been broken and that I won't have to go through it again. God showed me because I didn't get it right the first time when my first son ran away I had to go through it again. Please take note, that God will allow you to revisit a situation over and over until you pass the test. You determine how long your trial is.

I AM FREE

CHAPTER 10

How Jezebel Relates To Today's Time

MATTHEW 10:16 (NKJV)

"Behold, I send you out as sheep in the midst of wolves. Therefore be wise as serpents and harmless as doves.

You may ask yourself how Jezebel relates to today's time since today is very different from the Bible times. As we know, this spirit operates through men and women. Just because Jezebel is a woman in the Bible, we must understand that the traits and characteristics function through a man or woman. This may be surprising to most, but all deliverances my husband and I have performed a Jezebel spirit has been in most people. There were cases where the person didn't have any demons and needed inner healing, but Jezebel was right there controlling the entire situation. Jezebel can enter into a person in multiple ways. Listed below are some examples. Some of these examples come from demons speaking through the person.

WAYS DEMONS ENTER A PERSON

1. Rape

2. Molestation

3. Intercourse (Soul Tie). One person had the demon, and because the person opened themself up to sex before marriage, the demon entered the person.

4. Incest

5. Rejection

6. Insecurity

A NARCISSISTIC PERSON IS A JEZEBEL

Most people know this spirit through a narcissistic person. Also, most of us have been with or around a narcissistic person. If you have, then you have seen Jezebel at its finest. I encountered this spirit in two relationships. Based on my experience, Jezebel has multiple levels. The first person (relationship A) was very controlling and manipulative. The second person (relationship B) was controlling, manipulative, and aggressive. Even though they had the same spirit, they operated differently with their control and manipulation.

FOR EXAMPLE:

In **Relationship A**, if I didn't do something he wanted, he would give me the silent treatment and wouldn't help me with anything. The silent treatment would last days and, in most cases, weeks. When he was ready to talk to me, he would come to get in the bed, have sex with me, and then go back to the den to sleep. The next day would continue as if we had been talking and had no problems. Then the cycle would repeat itself if I didn't do something he wanted or if I did something he thought I shouldn't have done.

One situation of this was I asked his parents for directions to an event we all had to be at. I remember him getting so mad at me. He said I should have asked him for the directions. So, of course, he gave me the silent treatment. We had counseling once, and he told the pastor/counselor that he used silent treatment as a punishment. I couldn't believe that he even said that. He said it so boldly and with so much confidence. I was constantly afraid of messing up and hoping it didn't result in silent treatment. In another situation, he took my car from me and hid it in his parent's garage, and I had to get

105

a court order to get it back. I had, had enough mental abuse, and I couldn't take it anymore.

Sitting here writing this book takes me back to a place of emotions. This person tried to break me mentally, physically, emotionally, and sexually. The person I was years before was no longer the person I was when I finally left the relationship. I can honestly say that God has saved me. I could write a whole book on this one relationship, and who knows what the Lord has in store for the future.

Relationship B, was a crazy relationship itself. This relationship took me for a total spin in reality. Of course, the relationship started well, but the crazy narcissistic traits wasted no time showing themselves. The type of control this person had over me was he accused me of looking at other men and doing things to get their attention. When I started working in the same office as him, one of the other male coworkers mentioned that I could store my food in his refrigerator. Without thinking, I said ok and thank you, and I put my lunch in there. Later on, the guy I was with told me he had a refrigerator and that I should use his. He showed jealousy right away in an unhealthy way. That was just the start of what was to come. One time we went out to a club to have a good time. We were dancing, drinking, and vibing. Moments later, he got mad and said I was looking at men. I had no idea what he was talking about. Especially since my focus was on him the whole night. These incidents got so out of control that they resulted in the police being called. Being with this guy put me in fear of looking at people "men," because of what he might say. I started walking with my head down so he wouldn't accuse me of undressing men with my eyes.

The last incident I will share is that of which was in house. We both were on the bed and he seemed to be falling asleep so out of respect I decided to sit on the floor. I was also trying to do my work (I was in college at the time), so I decided to reposition my seating. As soon as I sat on the floor, I was accused of sitting on the floor so that I could message a man. He said that he saw me switch the screen to another screen as soon as he moved. Moments later, a car rides by his house and stops next to my car. Then I was accused of having someone over at his house while he was gone. He said, " What man have you had at my house." Then he explained what he saw the car doing. This type of control was scary. I would like to say that the abuse/control didn't stop here but it got worse. He later rapes me multiple times and stalks me, which was discussed in my first book "My Journey To Salvation" (Which can be purchased on Amazon).

As you see in both relationships, they both were controlling and manipulative but in two different ways. One was mentally abusive/controlling, and the other was verbally and physically controlling. Going through both experiences has taught me viable lessons.

Here are some traits I came in contact with when dealing with this spirit rather than if I was in a relationship, performing deliverance, or encountered it with an individual from church.

In Relationships:

1. Controlling

2. Promotes fear.

3. Manipulative

4. It causes you to walk away from your calling and purpose.

5. Lustful

6. Causes intrusive thoughts.

7. Envy

8. Greed

9. Causes mental strongholds.

10. If you do something they don't like, they will make you pay for it.

11. They can persuade people to make you look like a liar.

12. They have fears of their own and use manipulation and control of others to cover them up.

13. Have some type of addiction, and in most cases, it's related to sex/porn or drugs/alcohol.

14. Like to be in charge.

15. It's all about self.

16. Prideful person.

17. They don't like to be embarrassed or have people in their business.

18. They overplay their cards.

In The Church:

1. Like getting close to leaders such as the pastor.

2. They are overly nice people to those who don't know who they are.

3. Have some type of addiction, and in most cases, it's related to sex/porn.

4. If they are found out, then they will try to destroy the person or get them out of the church.

5. They don't like to be around people that are prophets and prophetess because God will reveal to them who they are.

6. They don't take advice and or prophecies that shed light on the truth within them.

7. Prideful person.

8. They are good at being number 2 because they are close to the person in charge. Typically they will get close enough to the pastor and start making the decisions, and the pastor will be blinded to what is happening.

9. They don't like to be embarrassed.

10. They overplay their cards.

11. Controlling

12. Lustful

13. Manipulative

14. Envy

15. Greed

16. Promotes fear.

17. They cause you to second-guess yourself.

18. Supportive to the one in a leadership position.

REMEMBER:

1. The person that has this spirit more than likely don't know that they have it.

2. They use control and manipulation to cover up the fears that they have. They are mostly coming from childhood and trauma.

3. The person's primary goal is to have control.

4. They get close to pastors and leaders.

5. They will attempt and, in most cases, remove the prophetic voice in the church.

6. If you expose Jezebel's spirit, the spirit will make people turn against you, and they will make you pay in any way that may hurt you emotionally and, in some cases, physically.

7. They are wolves in sheep's clothing.

8. Their words only matter.

9. If a woman has this spirit, she will try to sleep with the pastor, and she will try to control her husband.

JEZEBEL IN THE CHURCH

I was up one night having some alone time with God, and God began to speak to me about pastors, and He gave me a prophetic word to give to certain pastors and leaders. Some of the prophetic messages were good, and some were a warning. As God delivered the warnings to me, I thought to myself, how will I give these messages? I had a small amount of fear come across me, but in obedience, I sent the messages out one by one at 2 in the morning. I asked God, "Who am I to deliver these messages"? I felt like these pastors knew more than me, and I felt like they wouldn't listen. I sent the messages out, and some of the messages were rejected. I still had a sense of peace because I knew I had done what God had told me to do. God also told me to deliver one particular message to another pastor face-to-face, which I did with the help of my husband. Knowing that I was dealing with Jezebel, I wanted to run from what God was telling me to do. Just like Jonah and Elijah in the Bible. Because I have dealt with this spirit multiple times in past relationships, I like to stay away from people that are operating with this spirit.

After delivering these messages to the two pastors, things began to change immediately. The pastor that is/was dealing with the spirit of Jezebel began to talk to the head pastor. I mentioned to my husband that God had shown me that we would be sat down eventually, and a few days later, my husband was told that he could no longer go forth with the curse-breaking prayer that he had planned for that Wednesday. Then, God told me that we would be pulled from teaching, and that's exactly what happened. My husband was removed from teaching that following Sunday. God began to show us that we had to leave the church due to the church was/is being operated under demonic influence. God had given us a warning before it took place. Jezebel wanted us out of the church and was going to do so by planting negative seeds in the senior pastor's ears.

Some people may not realize that if you are in a church and Jezebel is present, you need to seek God in prayer and fasting and ask Him what to do about the situation. In most cases, God will tell you to leave because when destruction hits the person and the church, you don't want to be present for that. It can and will roll over to your life.

Revelation 2:20-23

> *20 But I have this [charge] against you, that you tolerate the woman Jezebel, who calls herself a prophetess [claiming to be inspired], and she teaches and misleads My bond-servants so that they commit [acts of sexual] immorality and eat food sacrificed to idols. 21 I gave her time to repent [to change her inner self and her sinful way of thinking], but she has no desire to repent of her immorality and refuses to do so. 22 [p]Listen carefully, I will throw her on a bed of sickness, and those who commit adultery with her [I will bring] into great anguish, unless they repent of her deeds. 23 And I will kill her children (followers) with [q] pestilence [thoroughly annihilating them], and all the churches will know [without any doubt] that I am He who searches the [r]minds and hearts [the innermost thoughts, purposes]; and I will give to each one of you [a reward or punishment] according to your deeds.*

What You Need To Understand Is:

1. If you tolerate this spirit, you will get the same punishment that Jezebel will receive.

2. The scripture in vs. 22 says you will be thrown on a bed of sickness if you commit adultery with her.

3. Vs. 23 mentions how people that follow the person with this spirit will receive pestilence.

4. God will give judgment where judgment is due.

- If you know that a person is operating with this spirit and you choose not to do anything about it, then you are agreeing with the spirit.

- If you have been warned about this spirit operating through a person and you choose to let them continue and not sit them down and talk with them, then you are agreeing with what they are doing.

- If you are allowing this spirit to control you, you are in agreement with this spirit (read vs. 20 over).

- If this is an apostle, pastor, or leader and the church don't sit the person down then they are agreeing with the spirit and will receive punishment.

This spirit must be confronted and exposed. God will send a warning to someone within the church and will give them insight into what is taking place. From what I have experienced the pastor didn't have the discernment that he once had because of this spirit. Jezebel is a very strong spirit (not stronger than God), and it must be dealt with immediately. This spirit will ruin an entire church if you don't catch it in the beginning. I was listening to one of my favorite pastors on YouTube and he said that if a Jezebel spirit is operating in the church and they are not being confronted, then you better run and take your family with you. Leave that church and don't look back. He also mentioned that God would give you dreams and visions and warnings of what is taking place, which was exactly what God was showing my husband and me. I want to encourage you to pray for your pastors and leaders and ask God to show you the hidden things within.

After my husband and I left the church, sadly to say it wasn't peaceful. We were removed from all platforms, and the people that we were ministering to were told they couldn't finish their sessions with us. Even to this day, there are a few people who don't talk to us. However, I do know that God will expose it all. There have been people coming to us and sharing things that they are now seeing since we have been gone and how the atmosphere has changed. There have been people that mentioned that they are struggling with certain things that they thought they were free from. When God removes the anointing of a church then the entire body of the church will suffer and possibly feel the wrath of God.

Anytime a person operates under any spirits and is speaking to the congregation, spirits are being released to the people. When people come to church, they are variable and ready to receive, which is why we have to pray and cover ourselves daily. Attacks come daily, so we need to be prepared daily by putting on the armor of God.

EPHESIANS 6:11-12

11 Put on the full armor of God, so that you can take your stand against the devil's schemes. 12 For our struggle is not against flesh and blood, but against the rulers, against the authorities, against the powers of this dark world and against the spiritual forces of evil in the heavenly realms.

WHAT IS THE FULL ARMOR?

1. Shoes of peace
2. Breastplate of righteousness
3. Sword of the spirit
4. Helmet of salvation
5. Belt of truth

This is something that I put on daily. I also pray and ask God to cover my kids with his armor. We have to stop the fiery darts that come our way. We have to stay grounded and rooted in Christ.

I am not sure what or who you are facing, but I want you to know that God will get you through. He will show you the way. You **MUST** put God in the midst of your situation, and you **MUST** fight this battle in the spiritual realm. As long as you fight this with your flesh, you will always lose the battle. God can go above and beyond what you can think or imagine. We **MUST** take God out of the box and prioritize Him over our lives.

QUESTIONS TO ASK YOURSELF

1. Who is controlling your life?
2. How and when did it start?
3. Was this relationship God ordained?
4. What scripture can you stand on to help you through this situation?
5. What fears have you gained from this relationship you need to renounce?

PRAYER

Father, I come to you today, and I ask for you to forgive me of (Fill in the blank). I also ask for forgiveness for any unknown sin. Thank you Father for being with me through all my trials, and I know that you will be there with me through the trials to come. I ask that you humble me so that I line up with your expectation for my life. Father, I ask that you teach me how to fight spiritually and not carnally. I ask that if there are any Jezebels in my life, please expose them to me right before my eyes. I ask that you remove any person that is monitoring my life. I ask that you give me the strength to leave people alone that are no good for me and that you give me new relationships with Godly people. I pray that my enemies' eyes are opened and that they receive a heart of love and compassion. I pray that they also have a heart of repentance. Lord, I ask that you remind me of your word when I get out of line. Father if I have grieved your spirit in any kind of way, I'm sorry and I repent and renounce my behavior. Father, I love you and honor you in Jesus's name Amen.

SALVATION PRAYER

Father, thank you for sending your son Jesus Christ to die on the cross for my sins. I ask for forgiveness for anything that I may have thought, said, or done. I ask that you cleanse me with Jesus's blood. I know that Jesus died on the cross for my sins and that he rose on the third day. I ask that His Spirit come and live on the inside of me to guide me, comfort me, convict me, and change me. Thank you, Father, for this amazing gift. In Jesus name I pray amen.

NOTES

CHAPTER 11

Scriptures To Stand On

JOHN 3:16 (NKJV)

"For God so [greatly] loved and dearly prized the world, that He [even] gave His [One and] [a]only begotten Son, so that whoever believes and trusts in Him [as Savior] shall not perish, but have eternal life.

As many of us know, when we are fighting a battle, we have to fight in the spiritual realm. Which means you will also have to fast and pray to God. God's word says that some spirits don't come out unless you are praying and fasting. I know there are areas in my life that I am still praying and fasting on. It doesn't matter how long it takes, but it does matter that we press into God daily. We have to shift our thinking, and we have to allow the Holy Ghost to have His way. As you go through your trials, I want you to highlight the scriptures that stand out to you the most and begin to use them in your battle.

Scriptures For Victory

Ephesians 6:10-17 (NKJV)

[10] Finally, my brethren, be strong in the Lord and in the power of His might. [11] Put on the whole armor of God, that you may be able to stand against the [a]wiles of the devil. [12] For we do not wrestle against flesh and blood, but against principalities, against powers, against the rulers of [b]the darkness of this age, against spiritual hosts of wickedness in the heavenly places. [13] Therefore take up the whole armor of God, that you may be able to withstand in the evil day, and having done all, to stand. [14] Stand therefore, having girded your waist with truth, having put on the breastplate of righteousness, [15] and having shod your feet with the preparation of the gospel of peace; [16] above all, taking the shield of faith with which you will be able to quench all the fiery darts of the wicked one. [17] And take the helmet of salvation, and the sword of the Spirit, which is the word of God;

Psalms 81:14 (NKJV)

I would soon subdue their enemies, And turn My hand against their adversaries.

Psalms 143:12 (NKJV)

In Your mercy cut[a] off my enemies, And destroy all those who afflict my soul; For I am Your servant.

LUKE 21:15 (NKJV)

For I will give you a mouth and wisdom which all your adversaries will not be able to contradict or [a]resist.

MICAH 5:9-15 (NLT)

9 The people of Israel will stand up to their foes, and all their enemies will be wiped out. 10 "In that day," says the LORD, "I will slaughter your horses and destroy your chariots. 11 I will tear down your walls and demolish your defenses. 12 I will put an end to all witchcraft, and there will be no more fortune-tellers. 13 I will destroy all your idols and sacred pillars, so you will never again worship the work of your own hands. 14 I will abolish your idol shrines with their Asherah poles and destroy your pagan cities. 15 I will pour out my vengeance on all the nations that refuse to obey me."

ZEPHANIAH 3:15 (NLT)

For the LORD will remove his hand of judgment and will disperse the armies of your enemy. And the LORD himself, the King of Israel, will live among you! At last your troubles will be over, and you will never again fear disaster.

DEUTERONOMY 30:7-8 (NLT)

7 The LORD your God will inflict all these curses on your enemies and on those who hate and persecute you. 8 Then you will again obey the LORD and keep all his commands that I am giving you today.

Psalms 6:10 (NLT)

May all my enemies be disgraced and terrified. May they suddenly turn back in shame.

Psalms 23:5-5 (NLT)

You prepare a feast for me in the presence of my enemies. You honor me by anointing my head with oil. My cup overflows with blessings.

Psalms 23:5-6 (NLT)

⁵ You prepare a feast for me in the presence of my enemies. You honor me by anointing my head with oil. My cup overflows with blessings. ⁶ Surely your goodness and unfailing love will pursue me all the days of my life, and I will live in the house of the LORD forever.

Psalms 31:1-5 (NLT)

¹ For the choir director: A psalm of David. O LORD, I have come to you for protection; don't let me be disgraced. Save me, for you do what is right. ² Turn your ear to listen to me; rescue me quickly. Be my rock of protection, a fortress where I will be safe. ³ You are my rock and my fortress. For the honor of your name, lead me out of this danger. ⁴ Pull me from the trap my enemies set for me, for I find protection in you alone. ⁵ I entrust my spirit into your hand. Rescue me, LORD, for you are a faithful God.

Psalms 9:3-6 (NKJV)

3 When my enemies turn back, They shall fall and perish at Your presence. 4 For You have maintained my right and my cause; You sat on the throne judging in righteousness. 5 You have rebuked the nations, You have destroyed the wicked; You have blotted out their name forever and ever. 6 O enemy, destructions are finished forever! And you have destroyed cities; Even their memory has perished.

Psalms 55:23 (NLT)

But you, O God, will send the wicked down to the pit of destruction. Murderers and liars will die young, but I am trusting you to save me.

Scriptures Against Fear and Doubt

Matthew 11:28-30 (NKJV)

28 "Come to Me, all [you] who labor and are heavy laden, and I will give you rest. 29 "Take My yoke upon you and learn from Me, for I am gentle and lowly in heart, and you will find rest for your souls. 30 "For My yoke [is] easy and My burden is light."

John 14:27 (NKJV)

"Peace I leave with you, My peace I give to you; not as the world gives do I give to you. Let not your heart be troubled, neither let it be afraid.

1 PETER 5:7 (NLT)

Give all your worries and cares to God, for he cares about you.

COLOSSIANS 3:15 (NLT)

And let the peace that comes from Christ rule in your hearts. For as members of one body you are called to live in peace. And always be thankful.

2 THESSALONIANS 3:16 (NKJV)

Now may the Lord of peace Himself give you peace always in every way. The Lord [be] with you all.

MATTHEW 6:25 (NLT)

"That is why I tell you not to worry about everyday life--whether you have enough food and drink, or enough clothes to wear. Isn't life more than food, and your body more than clothing?

PSALMS 55:22 (NLT)

Give your burdens to the LORD, and he will take care of you. He will not permit the godly to slip and fall.

PHILIPPIANS 4:6-7 (NKJV)

⁶ Be anxious for nothing, but in everything by prayer and supplication, with thanksgiving, let your requests be made known to God; hope. ⁷ and the peace of God, which surpasses all understanding, will guard your hearts and minds through Christ Jesus.

125

PROVERBS 12:25 (NKJV)

Anxiety in the heart of man causes depression, But a good word makes it glad.

SCRIPTURES ON FORGIVENESS

COLOSSIANS 3:13-14 (NKJV)

[13] *bearing with one another, and forgiving one another, if anyone has a complaint against another; even as Christ forgave you, so you also [must do.]* [14] *But above all these things put on love, which is the bond of perfection.*

MATTHEW 6:34 (NKJV)

"Therefore do not worry about tomorrow, for tomorrow will worry about its own things. Sufficient for the day [is] its own trouble.

PSALMS 23:4 (NKJV)

Yea, though I walk through the valley of the shadow of death, I will fear no evil; For You [are] with me; Your rod and Your staff, they comfort me.

PROVERBS 3:5-7 (NKJV)

[5] *Trust in the LORD with all your heart, And lean not on your own understanding;* [6] *In all your ways acknowledge Him, And He shall direct your paths.* [7] *Do not be wise in your own eyes; Fear the LORD and depart from evil.*

Jeremiah 17:7-8 (NKJV)

7 *"Blessed [is] the man who trusts in the LORD, And whose hope is the LORD.* 8 *For he shall be like a tree planted by the waters, Which spreads out its roots by the river, And will not fear when heat comes; But its leaf will be green, And will not be anxious in the year of drought, Nor will cease from yielding fruit.*

Isaiah 41:10-14 (NKJV)

10 *Fear not, for I [am] with you; Be not dismayed, for I [am] your God. I will strengthen you, Yes, I will help you, I will uphold you with My righteous right hand.'* 11 *"Behold, all those who were incensed against you Shall be ashamed and disgraced; They shall be as nothing, And those who strive with you shall perish.* 12 *You shall seek them and not find them-- Those who contended with you. Those who war against you Shall be as nothing, As a nonexistent thing.* 13 *For I, the LORD your God, will hold your right hand, Saying to you, 'Fear not, I will help you.'* 14 *"Fear not, you worm Jacob, You men of Israel! I will help you," says the LORD And your Redeemer, the Holy One of Israel.*

Jeremiah 29:11-12 (NKJV)

11 *For I know the thoughts that I think toward you, says the LORD, thoughts of peace and not of evil, to give you a future and a hope.* 12 *Then you will call upon Me and go and pray to Me, and I will listen to you.*

LUKE 23:34 (NKJV)

Then Jesus said, "Father, forgive them, for they do not know what they do." And they divided His garments and cast lots.

PSALMS 32:5 (NLT)

Finally, I confessed all my sins to you and stopped trying to hide my guilt. I said to myself, "I will confess my rebellion to the LORD." And you forgave me! All my guilt is gone. Interlude

JAMES 5:16 (NKJV)

Confess [your] trespasses to one another, and pray for one another, that you may be healed. The effective, fervent prayer of a righteous man avails much.

LUKE 6:37 (NKJV)

"Judge not, and you shall not be judged. Condemn not, and you shall not be condemned. Forgive, and you will be forgiven.

EPHESIANS 4:31-32 (NKJV)

[31] Let all bitterness, wrath, anger, clamor, and evil speaking be put away from you, with all malice. [32] And be kind to one another, tenderhearted, forgiving one another, even as God in Christ forgave you.

MATTHEW 6:14-15 (NKJV)

[14] *"For if you forgive men their trespasses, your heavenly Father will also forgive you.* [15] *"But if you do not forgive men their trespasses, neither will your Father forgive your trespasses.*

PROVERBS 17:9 (NKJV)

He who covers a transgression seeks love, But he who repeats a matter separates friends.

MATTHEW 18:21-22 (NKJV)

[21] *Then Peter came to Him and said, "Lord, how often shall my brother sin against me, and I forgive him? Up to seven times?"* [22] *Jesus said to him, "I do not say to you, up to seven times, but up to seventy times seven.*

ISAIAH 43:25-26 (NKJV)

[25] *"I, [even] I, [am] He who blots out your transgressions for My own sake; And I will not remember your sins.* [26] *Put Me in remembrance; Let us contend together; State your [case,] that you may be acquitted.*

SCRIPTURES ON PATIENCE

ROMANS 12:12 (NKJV)

Rejoicing in hope, patient in tribulation, continuing steadfastly in prayer;

129

EPHESIANS 4:2 (NLT)

Always be humble and gentle. Be patient with each other, making allowance for each other's faults because of your love.

PHILIPPIANS 4:6 (NKJV)

Be anxious for nothing, but in everything by prayer and supplication, with thanksgiving, let your requests be made known to God;.

GALATIANS 6:9 (NKJV)

And let us not grow weary while doing good, for in due season we shall reap if we do not lose heart.

JEREMIAH 29:11 (NKJV)

For I know the thoughts that I think toward you, says the LORD, thoughts of peace and not of evil, to give you a future and a hope.

PSALMS 37:7-9 (NKJV)

7 Rest in the LORD, and wait patiently for Him; Do not fret because of him who prospers in his way, Because of the man who brings wicked schemes to pass. 8 Cease from anger, and forsake wrath; Do not fret--[it] only [causes] harm. 9 For evildoers shall be cut off; But those who wait on the LORD, They shall inherit the earth.

Made in the USA
Columbia, SC
28 June 2024

37849220R00076